D1504525

BOOKS BY ROBERT S. DE ROPP

Drugs and the Mind

Science and Salvation

Man Against Aging

The Master Game

The New Prometheans

Church of the Earth

Warrior's Way

SELF-COMPLETION

Keys
to the
Meaningful
Life

Robert S. de Ropp

GATEWAYS/IDHHB, INC.
PUBLISHERS

Frontispiece photo by Eric Wynter

Diagrams by Kelly Rivera

Published by:
GATEWAYS / IDHHB, INC.
PO Box 370
Nevada City, CA 95959

ISBN: 0-89556-053-4
Library of Congress Card Catalog Number: 87-082943

Man should not ask what he may expect from life,
but should rather understand
that life expects something from him.

— Viktor Frankl, The Doctor and the Soul (1)

Advice from a Fool to a Mad King

Have more than thou showest;
Speak less than thou knowest . . .

— Shakespeare, King Lear, Act I, Scene 4

Table of Contents

III. THE REAL WORK

Introduction

On a mountainside in Northern California there lived, until his death in the Fall of 1987, a man who in this last book has something urgent to say to every person who is pursuing the inner-transformative path. This man introduces himself as a hermit. He also happens to be a distinguished research scientist, an internationally-known author and a veteran of decades of social, ecological and communitarian experiment with groups of seekers.

Robert S. de Ropp was a household name among the "counterculture" of the sixties: his book *The Master Game* burst upon a naive reading public carrying the data that there *are* schools in the West and there *is* access to mastery on the spiritual path from where we stand.

While the young were beginning to be captivated by shamanism in its most exotic and ethnic dress, of Native American, Asian, Australian practitioners, Robert de Ropp was already presenting his antidote to spiritual daydreams. His was a nitty-gritty, no-nonsense, de-mystifying, contemporary and scientifically-informed approach.

Most of the students who sought me out for serious guidance in the sixties and seventies had read and studied *The Master Game*. Astonishingly, the book sold several hundred thousand copies in paperback, because of the tenor of the times. An entire generation of readers who had not heard of Gurdjieff and Ouspensky from Colin Wilson or any other source—it was an insider secret well into the sixties that Europeans Gurdjieff and Crowley had achieved mastery on their own paths—first read these names in Robert de Ropp's book.

In the late eighties, all of that is forgotten. Literacy in general is on the wane, even as the alleged "new age" is on the rise. *The Master Game* is out of print. So are those other titles, *Church of the Earth*, *Drugs and the Mind* and *Warrior's Way*, Mr. de Ropp's own favorite. G.I. Gurdjieff and P.D. Ouspensky, Mr. de Ropp's original mentor, are now widely known, or widely subjects of lip service. So are all the 20th century living or dead Zen masters, Yogis, Gurus, Avatars, Swamis of every stamp.

Spiritual work, in fact, is "in" now. Meditation, transformation, levitation, clairvoyance, spirit communication— every psychic or hypnotic fantasy sort of superstition about other realities is current, chic. Only cogitation is still almost universally rejected and scarcely used. If anything, it is becoming further atrophied by the "new age."

In the midst of this revivalist fervor, Robert de Ropp's voice, from his hermitage on the mountainside, still sounds the same note. His message is distilled to its essence in *Self-Completion*. It addresses the same crisis he addressed in the sixties, with the same sense of urgency. More than a doomsayer, far more than a scientific observer, beyond the limitations of a utopian dreamer, Robert de Ropp speaks out with the integrity and acerbity of an old Testament prophet.

His message has aged like the finest wine, which is to say, it has achieved a superior bouquet for the eighties. This present summary is as candid and quintessential as any post-literate American could wish. It is addressed in particular to those already involved in spiritual work, a growing subculture. Every one on the spiritual path—no matter under what banner or practice—needs to read this book.

Anyone who is in an esoteric school needs to read it and study it carefully. Anyone who professes to be in the Work, no matter what the organizational affiliation or lineage, needs to read it at least three times and take its questions to heart. Anyone who professes to be a student of *mine*, anyone who indicates to me a wish to enter the Work, had better read it several more times and not mechanically, not just to "take notes".

If Mr. de Ropp's mental and emotional castor oil does not cause some misgiving—and if his summary of the beginning transformational work and the projection for possible success does not awaken some remorse of conscience in the reader—then that reader needs to examine his or her life.

Gnothe seauton — one who is indifferent to *Self-Completion* and its ideas may be closer to walking death-in-life than he or she is willing to acknowledge. Robert deRopp is gone, his writings and his work in this life are complete. But be forewarned: it may not be too late for you to choose life and assume the requisite responsibilities. Read this book at your own risk.

E.J. Gold

To the Reader

Greetings!

I am an elderly hermit who lives on the side of a mountain in California. I share this mountain with deer, skunks, opossums, rabbits, hawks, mice, vultures, redwoods, oaks, pepperwoods, grasses, not to mention about a zillion nematodes, fungi, bacteria. I am part of a complex ecosystem, a very small part I might add, a member of a trouble-making species, a naked ape that has become the bane of the biosphere because it has failed to find its proper place in the scheme of things.

In the basic construction of Man (2) something seems to have gone wrong.

Of this wrongness I have been aware since I was four. I was born in 1913, the last year of the Age of Optimism. I had scarcely been weaned before the proud tower of Western civilization, which many thought would enable mankind to ascend to a new heaven of health and material prosperity, collapsed with a crash. For me, a little child, that crash was symbolized by a piece of charred cloth which my father brought back to our flat in Chelsea, London. He was in the British Military Intelligence (he spoke English, French, German and Russian). He had been investigating the wreckage of a Zeppelin which had been shot down over London. He announced with a certain relish that the hydrogen-filled Zeppelins were death traps, specially designed to roast their crews alive. They served to prove, as he had always contended, that the Germans were fundamentally a stupid people, despite their major contributions to the arts and sciences.

His general comments passed over my head. My horrified attention was focussed on that piece of charred cloth, on the thought that a man's body had been in that uniform and that that man had been *roasted alive.* My father, instead of expressing grief, seemed to derive satisfaction from the fact.

As I gazed at the pile of Zeppelin wreckage spread out on our table the "terror of the situation" struck me like a physical blow. For three hours I wept, nor would any explanations my father offered (that the roasted Zeppeliner had been an enemy, that the Germans who made the raids were barbarous, and so on) banish from my childish soul the essential horror. For I realized at that early age that I had strayed onto the wrong planet in the wrong solar system, that the behavior of human beings was hopelessly and incurably weird, that I would always be an outcast among them, a "stranger in a strange land", an exile, an outsider.

Which indeed I was and still am. When Colin Wilson wrote his brilliant study, *The Outsider*, (3) I recognized at once how well that label fitted me. I had been an outsider from birth and would die an outsider. Never would I be able to accept gracefully or gratefully my membership of the human race. I would rather be a dolphin.

What are we, the outsiders? Are we the elect or the accursed? Are we the spiritual advance guard of the human race or a rabble of sorry misfits? We carry a heavy burden. We are the "sick souls" so well described by William James. (4) Our malaise can be summarized in the words of Cardinal Newman.

"To consider the defeat of the good, the prevalence of sin, the dreary, hopeless irreligion...all this a vision to dizzy and appall, and inflicts upon the mind the sense of profound mystery which is absolutely beyond human solution. And so I argue: If there be a God, the human race is implicated in some terrible, aboriginal calamity." (5)

Carrying the burden of this awareness, we, the outsiders, are always in danger. How many of us have voluntarily left the theater of life in disgust or despair, taking refuge in insanity or suicide? Like Ivan Karamazov we often hasten to give back our entrance ticket. We say to the Creator-God, "If this is the best you can do then I want out."

So it was with me. I was young, healthy, curious, a student of biology at the University of London, eager to do research. But the spectacle of the large-scale idiocy took away my appetite for life. God's creation, in general, seemed admirable, but he had evidently made a mess of things when he made Man. What I really wanted was to live in a man-free world. As this was impossible I decided that I would hand back my entrance ticket and hope to reincarnate in a species less badly constructed.

I might indeed have handed back the ticket had I not, at the age of twenty-three, met the man who was to be my teacher, P.D. Ouspensky. It was from Ouspensky I learned the vital secret. Man, as he is, is an uncompleted being. Nature provides for his development up to a point. He spends "twenty years agrowing and twenty years in bloom, twenty years declining and twenty years adying." He is a long lived mammal but does not understand why Nature has given him such a long life. Nature has not, generally speaking, made any attempt to provide him with this knowledge. Indeed she seems to have made every effort to conceal from him the real purpose of his existence.

But what we call Nature is a very mysterious force. It seems to operate at two levels, a lower and a higher. Lower Nature presides over Man's physical growth, brings him to maturity, turns on the sex urge that drives him to mate and, in due course, destroys him. But there is also a higher Nature. Higher Nature has given to Man the capacity to raise his level on the Great Chain of Being. In order to do this Man must first realize that he is not complete. It is part of his duty to complete himself. This work of self-completion involves two things, knowledge and effort.

To obtain the necessary knowledge, Ouspensky explained, and to use that knowledge for self-completion, was the proper purpose of human life. This was the *magnum opus contra naturae*, the "Great Work against Nature" of the alchemists. The alchemists had disguised their knowledge. They pretended that they sought a method of converting base metals into gold. But the real aim of alchemy was self-completion. This was "the Work". For those in the know, it was the only life game worth playing.

Unfortunately this great truth was understood by only a few people in each generation. These people strove, as it was said, to "enter the Work". This involved finding a teacher and getting the knowledge needed to enable them to work on themselves.

The mass of mankind were quite uninterested in the Work. They lived in a manner unworthy of their spiritual heritage, in the satisfaction of animal appetites, in fear, vanity, distractions and amusements, in stupid sports, games of skill and chance, greed of gain, fear of loss, dull daily work, the dreams and hopes of the day. They moved in obedience to forces over which they had no control. As soon as they stopped obeying one force they began obeying another.

The civilization of our time, declared Ouspensky, was a pale, sickly growth that could hardly keep itself alive in the darkness of profound barbarism. The technical inventions of the modern age had probably taken away from civilization more than they had given. (6)

In their incompleted state human beings thought they were awake when they were really moving about in a state of hypnotized sleep. They thought they had will but they had no real will. They thought they were free but they were really slaves. They thought they had something they called "I" but they had no real I, only a multitude of petty selves with different desires and different aims.

In their state of "waking sleep" humans voyaged from birth to death aboard a ship of fools. The captain was asleep, the steersman was drunk and the navigator had forgotten the aim of the voyage. Any fool on board could push the steersman aside and try to steer the ship. The great human agglomerates that called themselves nations were just as much at the mercy of the fools in their midst as were individual men and women. The technological Titanic, modern society, was proceeding full speed ahead into the fog, but there was *no one in control*. Under these circumstances it would not be surprising if the vessel hit a rock or an iceberg. The surprising thing was that it stayed afloat at all.

Ouspensky's teachings offered little comfort and at first I refused to accept them. But the crimes and stupidities of the "Dirty Thirties" compelled me finally to accept Ouspensky's view of the human predicament. By 1936 it was evident to any impartial observer that something had gone terribly wrong. I was half German, product of a long line of Baltic Barons (Germans with Russian souls). I had a large collection of German cousins. They were, whether they liked it or not, involved with the Nazis. Several were members of the Party. The tales they told appalled me. A whole procession of spiritually malformed monsters was emerging from the Teutonic collective unconscious. No crime was too heinous, no lie too preposterous for these new "supermen".

Obviously these monsters were a menace and needed to be chased back into the cesspool from which they had emerged. But the victors of World War I, British and French alike, seemed paralyzed. They did nothing. All the sacrifices of the first World War had been in vain. No one had learned anything. The whole idiotic war would have to be fought over again.

Our modern world, technically so proficient, was actually an example of the "theater of the absurd". The performance made no sense whatever.

So I studied with Ouspensky. I searched for a clue, for some way out of the "abyss of meaninglessness". Paul Tillich, at that time, had yet to write *The Courage to Be* but the thought he later expressed in that book described my situation entirely. "If life is as meaningless as death, if guilt is as questionable as perfection, if being is no more meaningful than nonbeing, on what can one base the courage to be?" (7)

Everything P.D. Ouspensky taught centered around a system. It was not just any old system. It was *the System*. He had received the System from his teacher, G. Gurdjieff, but he considered it incomplete, "fragments of an unknown teaching". Either Mr. G., as he called him, had not known the complete system or he had chosen not to reveal it in its entirety. Ouspensky had broken with Gurdjieff and forbidden any of us to make contact with that teacher. If we wanted to find the missing parts of the System we would have to discover them for ourselves. (8)

The System, if one understood it fully, would explain everything, from the origin of the universe to the peculiarities of human behavior. Everything was linked to everything else in a chain of interdependent cosmoses which ranged from the megalocosmos to the microcosmos. Each cosmos was governed by its own laws. The cosmos above imposed laws on the cosmos below. Man, the microcosmos, lived under laws imposed by the cosmos above him. This cosmos was Earth's organic life, the biosphere. The biosphere as a whole lived under laws imposed by the Sun. The Sun was governed by laws imposed by the Galaxy and so on.

It was also true to say that the cosmos above was influenced by the cosmos below. In Man the cosmos below was the cell. Man as a whole imposed laws on his cells. His instinctive brain regulated their rate of division, differentiation, metabolism and so on. As long as his cells obeyed these laws there was harmony and order. If they refused to obey, as in a cancer, chaos resulted. Similarly, the individual organisms of the biosphere lived under laws imposed by this cosmos and had the power to damage that cosmos, perhaps fatally, if they refused to obey its laws.

The separate links in the chain of cosmoses were held together by the law of reciprocal feeding. Radiation from the Sun nourished the cosmos of green plants which in turn nourished the animals, including Man. Every cosmos was food for the cosmos above it and fed in its turn on products of the cosmos below.

For what, in this "Great Chain of Being" was Man the food? According to the System Man was potentially "food for Archangels". Just what these Archangels were was never explained. In any case Man rarely fulfilled his true function. To become food for Archangels Man first had to complete himself. Few human beings did this. Instead of being food for Archangels Man was more often merely "food for Moon".

In the System, as propounded by Ouspensky, a lot of emphasis was placed on the role of the Moon. In the "Ray of Creation" the Moon was the growing end of a branch. Far from being a cold, dead body the Moon was getting bigger and warmer. It grew by feeding. On what did it feed? On the organic life of Earth. Everything living on Earth was food for the Moon. All the movements and manifestations of people, animals and plants were controlled by the Moon. The mechanical part of a man's life was regulated by the Moon. Only those who developed in themselves consciousness and will could escape from its power. The Moon was the "outer darkness" of the Christian teachings, the end of the world where there will be "weeping and gnashing of teeth". (9)

Being in those days a starry-eyed believer I took this moon-myth seriously. I actually saw the Moon, hanging there in the sky, as a sinister man-eating monster sucking from Earth's organic life its vital juices, slowly growing and warming itself at our expense.

Later, disillusioned not only with Ouspensky but with most of the so-called System, I rejected the "Gurdjieffian Lunar Myth" as a piece of cosmological nonsense. How could anyone seriously claim that the Moon was growing and getting warmer? Men had travelled to the Moon, walked on its surface, brought back moon-rocks. The Moon was dead. There was not the slightest chance of its coming to life. The whole idea of the "Ray of Creation" was incorrect. The cosmos did not grow like a tree. New stars were formed out of the dust and gas in the spiral arms of the galaxies. Old stars died, the small ones shrinking into white dwarfs, the big ones exploding as supernovas. Out of the dust of those supernovas new stars were formed.

Of course it was perfectly possible to argue that the whole moon-myth was an allegory, that the entity "moon" had no reference to the Moon in the sky. It described all those forces that work to keep Man enslaved and which prevent him from seeing the truth about his situation. But why disguise the truth in such an elaborate allegory? It only served to confuse people.

So the System, as we received it from Ouspensky, was a weird mixture. When it came to describing the predicament of Man, the forces that kept Man in sleep, the methods by which he could awaken, the System was wonderfully practical and down to earth. But when it came to describing the laws governing cosmic processes it seemed to lose touch with reality. It became wooly, a mish-mash of fantasy. It reminded me of the colorful myths that play such an important part in the writings of H.P. Blavatsky. Both Gurdjieff and Ouspensky claimed to despise Theosophy but I suspected that Gurdjieff had been strongly influenced by certain Theosophical ideas.

Another item in Ouspensky's teaching the truth of which I came to question concerned an entity he called "the inner circle of humanity". When I first met him he firmly believed that that circle existed. Its members were the custodians of the "culture of civilization" which was opposed to the "culture of barbarism" that prevailed in the world at large.

This idea of an inner circle was not new to me. I had come to Ouspensky heavily loaded with the jargon of the Theosophical Society of which, at the time, I was a member. Among the items contained in what I now call "The Great Theosophical Myth" was the concept of the Masters of Wisdom. It was the Mahatma Letters allegedly sent by one of those Masters (Koot Hoomi) that formed so important a part of the bag of tricks of Helena Blavatsky, founder of the Theosophical Society. (10)

Ouspensky had nothing but scorn for Theosophy. "I wouldn't touch it with a barge pole." But he did believe in the existence of the "inner circle". Members of the circle constituted a spiritual aristocracy. They were developed beings. They had will, inner unity, permanent I. They were self-directing entities, not mechanical dolls.

But if these marvellous characters really existed why did they hide themselves? Obviously they did stay hidden. They certainly made no effort to save mankind from the results of its folly.

Ouspensky answered this question by insisting that the members of the inner circle could only help those who wished to be helped. Nor could they help anyone who was not willing to help himself. The mass of mankind were slaves who did not know they were slaves and therefore had no desire to be free. Attempts to liberate them from their slavery often proved disastrous for the would-be liberators.

That seemed true enough. Look what had happened to Jesus! See what a mess the priests had made of his teachings! You start with a religion of love and end with Inquisitors who burn their fellow men alive. The history of Christianity offered a horrendous example of the workings of the Theater of the Absurd.

Members of the inner circle, said Ouspensky, were far too intelligent to let themselves get mixed up in this ridiculous performance. They stepped back and watched the show. If a few people wanted to do more with their lives than take part in a drama of absurdities they might approach the inner circle, assuming they could find it. After a long period of work on themselves they might become worthy to enter the circle. It was no easy undertaking. (11)

"It takes a long time to enter the Work. One must be patient."

Thus spake P.D. Ouspensky one foggy December afternoon in the fateful year 1936.

I write now in January 1987. Fifty years have passed since I heard Ouspensky's words.

"It is hard to enter the Work. Many start, few arrive."

Why?

This question echoes through my head. Why is this inner Work so difficult? Have we, in our materialistic culture, blocked ourselves off from certain life-giving influences that could help us? There surely are such influences but they seem to reach only a very few people. These people know a great secret. They know they are unfinished beings and that it is up to them to complete their own evolution. They see mankind as the choice fruit of the Tree of Life on Earth but they know that, in most cases, the fruit falls from the tree unripe. Man, who should become food for higher beings, becomes instead food for worms. He drifts down instead of rising up. He fattens his flesh instead of nourishing his soul.

Those who receive these influences have the opportunity, if they so desire, to enter the inner circle of humanity. They are the gnostics, those who know. But their knowledge will accomplish nothing unless it provides a basis for action. Actually it is better to be ignorant than to know and do nothing with one's knowledge. But what must one do?

This is the vital question. One must *know* and one must *do*. In order to do one must generate power.

Power is developed by effort, but there is right effort and wrong effort. There is also pseudo-effort. Our capacity for self-deception is very great and it continues to operate after we have, as we imagine, "entered the Work". Instead of engaging in the real Work we enter the fantasy Work. We deceive ourselves. Our last state is worse than our first.

This, after fifty years of observation, is the conclusion I have reached. The fantasy Work tends to replace the real Work just as, according to Gresham's Law, the bad money tends to drive out the good. The fantasy Work is everywhere. It proliferates like a cancer. It is subtle. It takes many forms. It generates new systems of delusions to replace the old ones. It brings the real Work to a halt and offers dreams in its place. Many people gladly accept those dreams. The dreams save the dreamers from making serious efforts to awaken because they dream that they are already awake.

All I can do at this late stage of my life is to offer a guide to those who need one. With the help of this guide they may be able to distinguish fantasy from reality. It is hard for those who have contacted only the feeble remnants of an enterprise that once had life and vigor to understand what real Work is. It is even harder for them to put that understanding into practice. There is not much we can do about this. The vital influence that the Sufis call *baraka* is now shut off from us by the fog of insane materialism that has enshrouded our culture. Our huge, unbalanced economy is a house of cards which will surely collapse. When it does the fog may clear and the vital influence may encounter fewer obstructions. Until that time we must do what we can with what we have and strive to distinguish between fantasy and reality.

I

GOD, MAN, COSMOS

Reality Seeking

What is the real world? Can we know it?

The answer to this question is no. We are cut off from the "world out there" by a barrier that cannot be surmounted. We can know only as much as our senses, aided by various instruments, enable us to know. We can be aware only of that portion of the world that our consciousness reveals.

Asleep in bed we enter the world of dreams, which may appear to us perfectly real at the time. Awake we enter the world we call real but that reality is very limited. Our senses construct a model of the world that enables us to function more or less effectively. It enables doctors to practice medicine, lawyers to practice law, garbage collectors to gather garbage, farmers to grow crops, airline pilots to guide aircraft.

Is this the real world? Obviously not. Reality, if this word has any meaning, includes all the events that occupy the cosmos from galaxies to atoms and all the interactions that take place between these entities. They are all connected in a single web and happenings at one level affect events at another.

What we commonly call reality is a tiny fraction of the big reality. It consists of a body with its needs, a mind with its needs, a mate with his or her needs, children with their needs, a job, an employer, a house, a car, a few streets, a store or two.

This is our little world, familiar, confining, dull. This is our "boss reality". It imposes laws on us that we break at our peril. We must drive on the proper side of the road. We must get to work on time. We must pay taxes and bills, buy groceries, send the children to school. We live under many laws. We are not free agents.

But what about alternative or separate realities? Is this dull micro-world of ours the only possible world? Obviously not. Endowed as we are with the capacity to fantasize we can construct any separate reality we like. If that reality conflicts too obviously with the boss reality we shall have to keep it to ourselves or run the risk of being thought mad, dangerous or both.

There are people who live in several worlds at the same time. William Blake saw at least two realities and sometimes as many as four.

Now I a fourfold vision see,
And a fourfold vision is given to me:
'Tis fourfold in my supreme delight
And threefold in soft Beulah's night
And twofold Always. May God us Keep
From Single vision and Newton's sleep!

What was this "single vision and Newton's sleep" from which Blake prayed that we might be delivered? It was the narrow world of the logician, the world a quantity. While it is perfectly correct to proclaim that two and two must equal four under all ordinary conditions, it is not true to say that every whole is merely the sum of its parts. Quality emerges from quantity. The higher holons are qualitatively different from the bits out of which they are assembled. Put the parts of a watch in a bag and shake them as long as you like. You will never get a functioning watch. But let a watchmaker exert his skill and behold a new holon. A mechanism has emerged from the parts that, by its movement, measures the flow of time.

What has the watchmaker done to produce this new entity? He has used his skill to impose on the parts a higher level of order. Each separate piece of the watch relates to every other piece in a special way. This is the only way in which it can relate if the new holon is to emerge.

An understanding of the real world can only be gained by those able to see the hierarchy of holons that make up that world. "Single vision and Newton's sleep" blinds us by placing too much emphasis on *quantities* and ignoring emergent *qualities*. The major emergent qualities in the Hierarchy of Being are *life* and *mind*. Neither life nor mind can be expressed in quantitative terms. There are no units in which either "lifeness" or "mindness" can be expressed. When we look at a living organism we are seeing a complex hierarchy of units, subatom, atom, molecule, macromolecule, organelle, organ, organism. Organisms are part of various ecosystems that together constitute the biosphere. The biosphere as a whole is linked to cosmic entities, planets, suns, galaxies, that support and nourish the system.

So, if we ask the question, "What is reality?", we can at least find an approximate answer. Reality is a hierarchy of increasingly complex holons. At a certain level of this hierarchy the Mind Force becomes conscious of itself and can begin to understand its own nature. The understanding acquired by such an embodied mind is limited by its ability to *see*. We use the word here as Blake uses it to imply a vision of the world at several levels.

"What?" it will be questioned, "When the sun rises do you not see a round disk of fire somewhat like a guinea?" "O no, no. I see an innumerable company of the Heavenly host crying, Holy, holy, holy is the Lord God Almighty. I question not my Corporeal or Vegetative Eye any more than I would

question a Window concerning a Sight. I look thru'
it not with it."

Blake was a gnostic. He could *see*. He saw beyond
the *creatura* into the *pleroma*. "If the doors of
perception were cleansed everything would appear
to man as it really is, infinite." It is just this
"cleansing of the doors of perception" that
constitutes the main task of those who would enter
the Work.

The Lattice of Karma

I AM HERE NOW.

I AM. The full awareness of my own being is
given to me only now and then. Why? Because,
much of the time, I am lost in fantasy. I am
definitely *not here now*. I am wandering around in
the past or dreaming about the future, or thinking
about something, speculating about something,
talking to someone who is not even there,
imagining, indulging. What a way to live!

But the full sense of the I AM comes to me when I
remember. With it comes awareness of place, the
HERE, and awareness of time, the NOW. And with
it too comes the sense of separation, the feeling of
being outside spacetime, an observer standing on
the bank of time's river and watching the flow. This
is *zikr*, remembering.

Self-remembering? But I have many selves. I am a
veritable ship of fools. Which self do I remember?

None of them. This Self is outside of spacetime,
the white bird, messenger of the *pleroma*, beyond
change, beyond death.

Pleroma and *creatura*, the two aspects of God... I am a creature, generated by the Life Force, which was generated by the Mind Force, which gave shape to the *creatura*. Among the multiplicity of worlds, among the ever growing swarm of sentient beings I seek the Creator, my Creator. Why? Because it is my right and my being-duty. In me the Creator has generated a mirror in which it could see itself. That mirror tends to get covered with dust and filth. Most of the time it reflects nothing. It is my job to wipe off the dust and filth. To do this I must remember. I must *be*.

I AM.

Reader, take it from me. Every step you take on the *true* Way (and I specify the true Way because there are dozens of false ones) leads to the I AM. But the way in which this I AM is experienced depends on the place we have reached on the Way. In the realm of the *creatura* the I AM can embrace the entire megalocosmos with all its worlds within worlds. This is called cosmic consciousness. The borders delimiting the separate self dissolve, lost in awareness of the greater whole.

It is also possible for the I AM to go beyond the *creatura*. It can blend with the *pleroma*, the Eternal Unchanging. This is the ultimate stage of the Way, the final liberation. Further than this we cannot go.

About the *pleroma* it is impossible to speak. About the *creatura* much can be said. Is it useful to say it? Yes, I maintain that it is useful. We need to understand the force that created us, that placed us here in these bodies, on this planet, in this solar system. We cannot lightly dismiss the *creatura*. We are part of it, a tiny thread in the Lattice of Karma. We want to know who we are, why we are, whence we came, where we are going. We cannot understand the significance of our own being unless we take into account the larger picture.

To understand one thing we must strive to understand everything because everything is connected to everything else.

This is the foundation of holistic thinking. Without such thinking we cannot create a meaningful model of the world in which we live. The purpose of this book, as stated in its subtitle, is to offer the reader keys to the meaningful life. Meaning cannot be found unless we consider the big picture.

Let us examine the implications of this statement. We can best do this by engaging in the meditation on the Lattice of Karma.

The Lattice of Karma is the web of cause and effect woven by the three forces on the loom of time. It can be examined from various angles. The further back one steps the more one can see of the general pattern but the less one sees of the details. Both the long distance view and the short distance view are needed.

Let me offer an example. We begin with the practical question, "Why am I here?". We go back step by step over the chain of interdependent causes. The steps can be very large or very small. Large steps are necessary if we are to see the whole picture.

So why am I here?

I am here because a certain sperm united with a certain ovum in the year 1912, nine months before I

was born. I am here because about 600,000 years
ago a hairy hominid (probably *Homo erectus*)
arrived in Europe from Africa and mutated into a
new form with a much larger brain. I am here
because, on the newly formed planet Earth about
4,000 million years ago three giant molecules which
we now call DNA, RNA and protein became
organized by the Life Force into the first living
things. I am here because about 4,650 million years
ago a giant star exploded in one of the spiral arms of
the Milky Way scattering into space all the 92
elements out of which the Solar System in which I
live was born. I am here because 12,500 million
years ago the great primordial gas cloud of
hydrogen and helium condensed into galaxies. I am
here because at Planck time (of which more later) a
something emerged from a *nothing* and that
something grew into a megalocosmos consisting of
maybe 100 billion galaxies each containing maybe a
hundred billion stars.

Reader, let me repeat my previous statement. It
cannot be overemphasized. If you really want to
understand one thing you must understand
everything. Everything depends on everything else.
We cannot understand our place in the scheme of
things unless we know something about the
megalocosmos.

Man is an actor in a cosmic drama. It is true that,
in most cases, he does not know his part and acts
very badly. But one thing seems certain. Man could
manage better if he knew what the play was all
about, who set the stage, who devised the plot.

Can we ever get such knowledge?

It is, I'll admit, a tall order. Our knowledge about these things will never be precise. We are forced to guess. We must create a working hypothesis. Scientists do this all the time. A working hypothesis provides the basis for experiments, and the experiments either confirm the hypothesis or they don't. If they don't a different hypothesis will be needed.

But a working hypothesis about the cosmic drama can never be tested by experiment. It is beyond our power to create an experimental megalocosmos. What we can do is to formulate the hypothesis we prefer and check it against the observed facts. If it does not square with the facts out it goes! This is why I rejected what I have called "the Gurdjieffian Lunar Myth" which concerns the role of the Moon and the growth of the "Ray of Creation". The idea is not supported by the evidence.

Scientists, Gnostics, Believers

We are talking now about knowledge, not about faith. Those who follow the Way of Faith are Believers. Those who follow the Way of Knowledge are either scientists or gnostics.

Believers will believe anything. The most fantastic myths, the most impossible miracles are swallowed by the Believers simply because "it is written in the Scriptures" or because the spiritual authority of their choice tells them that such myths and miracles are true.

The gnostics and scientists have no use for belief. They want to *know*. But scientific knowledge and the *gnosis* are somewhat different. The gnostic accounts for this difference by separating the "knowledge of the heart", the *gnosis cardias*, from the "knowledge of the head". (12)

The scientist is concerned entirely with the "knowledge of the head". It guides him in his researches. It is applicable to all those situations in which a hypothesis can be verified by experiment. Suppose we ask, "Does light consist of waves or particles?". We perform certain experiments. As a result we conclude that light consists of waves. We perform other experiments. They indicate that light consists of packets of energy or quanta. So we conclude that light is both waves and particles, wavicles if you will. This is a somewhat surprising finding but it answers our question, "What is light?".

But suppose we ask some more abstruse questions. Did the universe start by accident or did it develop according to a plan? Was life on Earth organized by some intelligent force or did it result from a chance combination of molecules in the primordial oceans? Was Man created intentionally to perform a certain task or is he merely an accidental product of random mutations sorted out by the sieve of natural selection? Experiments will not provide answers to these questions. We are forced to guess.

The gnostics claim that the correctness of these guesses depends on our use of the "knowledge of the heart". "Knowledge of the heart" is not the same thing as religious belief. Gnostics are not believers. They *know*. But they cannot account for certain aspects of their knowledge. It comes to them from the sacred *sophia*, the divine spark. It results from their capacity, acquired by practice, to look into the core of things with the "eye of enlightenment". All human beings possess that eye but only the gnostics know how to use it. This enables the gnostics to look directly into the mysterious forces that have shaped the cosmic drama.

Does this mean that the gnostics have no use for the evidence provided by modern science? It means nothing of the sort. A conscientious modern gnostic takes care to keep himself informed about every major finding that bears on the central questions.

What are the central questions? They can be stated very simply. What is the proper function of Man on the planet Earth? What role is he supposed to play in the cosmic drama? If, as the evidence suggests, he has been left by Nature uncompleted, how can he complete himself? If he lives in sleep how can he learn to awaken? If he is a slave how can he become free?

Contemporary science has practically nothing to say about any of these questions. They are dealt with by the science of metapsychology which, in other cultures, was considered to be the queen of the sciences. It is neglected in our culture which is narrow, shallow and grossly materialistic, but it remains a very important branch of science. No one can live a truly meaningful life without its aid.

God, Sophia, Demiurge

Reader, allow me at this point to back track a little. A slight digression is called for, a brief trip

into the past. We are, after all, the inheritors of
many spiritual traditions and are bound to take
those traditions into account. We did not spring into
spacetime with empty minds like the goddess
Athena from the head of Zeus. A thousand voices
clamor in us, the voices of the dead, who sought for
answers which they failed to find. What was that
message which C.G. Jung heard so distinctly when
the dead crowded around his house in Kussnacht?
(13)

*We have come back from Jerusalem where we
found not what we sought.*

Stuffy, antiquated, dogma-ridden Jerusalem,
home of the Pharisee and the High Priest, was
tightly enclosed in its fortress-like walls of dogma
and ritual. So the dead found nothing in Jerusalem
and came to Jung. Jung was a spiritual descendant
of the proto-gnostics who lived in the city of
Alexandria on the Nile delta ("the city where East
meets West"). It was a city open to every wind that
blew and every doctrine that circulated in those
early days (second century A.D.) before the
Christian Church had placed its fetters on the
human mind.

So Jung offered to the dead his *Seven Sermons*,
not in his own name but in the name of Basilides,
one of the great proto-gnostics of Alexandria. And
we, who aspire to the title of neo-gnostics, should at
least acquaint ourselves with the views of those old
heretics who are, in a sense, our spiritual ancestors.
(14)

So we will briefly outline the theories of the old
gnostics of the Alexandrian school and of the

Eastern school in India. We will then give a more detailed account of the ideas of the neo-gnostics. These ideas relate to the process of creation and offer answers to the question, "Why am I here?". Our aim is to construct a meaningful cosmos and to find the place Man occupies in the scheme of things.

In the beginning, said the gnostics of Alexandria, there was the Mind Force, the *nous*. The Mind Force was all pervading. It was the "God outside Creation", beyond time, beyond space, beyond matter and energy. How can one describe such a being? The proto-gnostics said it was impossible. This entity was inconceivable to our minds. Nonetheless they had names for it. Even the indescribable had to be called something. They called it "the Alien", "the Other", "the Unknown", "the Nameless", "the Hidden", "the Unknown Father".

Why Father? Why not Mother? A hard question. Talking about the Father God had become something of a habit in the second century and the gnostics adopted that habit.

In the beginning the Mind was unmanifest. It was the *pleroma*, the fullness. Within the *pleroma* there existed an infinity of universes, but they existed only in potential. Modern physicists like to describe this state of infinite potential as a sort of "quantum foam". Do the physicists really know what they are talking about? Probably not, and at least one of them, James Peebles, has had the grace to admit it. "What the universe was like at day number minus one, before the big bang, one has no idea. The

equations refuse to tell us, I refuse to speculate."
(15)

It might have been a good idea if the proto-gnostics had shared this sensible attitude. They did no such thing. They speculated and speculated and *speculated*. Simon Magus, Basilides, Valentinus, Carpocrates, the unknown writer now called Hermes Trismegistus, all strove to describe the indescribable. As a result the *pleroma*, the unmanifested, beyond time, beyond space, beyond matter, began to swarm with mysterious entities. What the modern physicists call a quantum foam was seen by the proto-gnostics as a ferment of activity centering around mythical figures having decidedly human characteristics.

The one indescribable unfathomable Silence generated the *nous* (Mind) and Mind in turn generated the *epinoia* or *ennoia* (Thought). Moreover, because Mind was active and Thought passive it was considered permissible to describe Mind as the Father and Thought as his female emanation. The original monad became a dyad. Mind and Thought were an androgyne, joined in unity yet ranged opposite each other. In this combination Mind was the power governing everything and male. Thought was the lower principle which brought forth everything and was considered female.

So the void, the original *pleroma*, began to differentiate. The entities that emerged were not material but existed in some strange middle world between the void and the creation.

Having postulated the dyad the imaginations of the proto-gnostics really took flight. It was Simon Magus, "the father of heresy", who set the ball rolling.

Simon was certainly an original character. Tradition has it that he travelled with a female companion, a girl called Helen whom he had picked up in a brothel in Tyre. Whether this is true or not we cannot tell but he had a very respectful attitude toward the female human which was unusual in a culture dominated by males. In any case he regarded his Helen as the embodiment of *sophia*, "God's erring wisdom", that had emerged from *ennoia* and strayed into the lower depths.

Sophia's error was due to a misunderstanding. She thought that "the Unknown Father outside Creation" intended to generate emanations from himself in the form of angels and archangels. So, descending into the lower regions, she anticipated the Father, and created the power (the Demiurge) by which the cosmos was made.

The Demiurge, according to the proto-gnostics, was a composite being consisting of seven Archons, the tyrannical guardians of the seven worlds. Sophia was detained by the Archons and dragged down by them from the highest heaven into the cosmos. She suffered all manner of abuse that she might not return upward to the Father. Enclosed in human flesh she migrated for centuries into different female bodies. She was, among other beings, the famed Helen over whom the Trojan war was fought. Migrating from body to body, suffering abuse in each, she finally became a whore in a brothel.

Thus spake Simon Magus, who appears to have originated the idea of *Sophia-Prunikos* , "Wisdom the Whore".

But why were the proto-gnostics so hated by those pillars of orthodoxy, the Fathers of the Church? They were hated because they dared to publish an awful truth. The Jewish Creator-God, which the Fathers of the Church had adopted (or stolen), was not God at all! That "God" was actually an arrogant, presumptuous Demiurge with seven aspects (the Archons), all of them repulsive. The Demiurge thought it was God. Of the real God, the Unknown Father, it had no idea.

The Creator-God of the Biblical Genesis was supposed to be all powerful, all knowing, all loving. The proto-gnostics declared that it was none of those things. It was a bungling tyrant. It did not even speak the truth. It told Adam and Eve that they would surely die if they ate of the fruit of the tree of knowledge of good and evil. But the snake came along and told them to eat of the fruit. They would not die, said the snake. On the contrary they would gain great knowledge. So they ate and did not die.

So much for that all knowing God! Adam and Eve, declared the proto-gnostics, rejected that God and worshipped the snake instead because it was the bringer of truth and wisdom.

The arrogant Archons who imagined that they were God imprisoned *sophia* (the divine spark) in a material form. That form was Adam, the first man, who, with his wife Eve, generated the human race. Adam and his descendants had the divine spark within them and could, if they knew how, escape from the bondage of the material world.

To keep them in bondage the tyrannical Archons intoxicated the children of Adam with the "wine of forgetfulness". This prevented them from recognizing the divine spark in themselves. They were rendered permanently drunk. They lived amid dreams and delusions. They forgot their high origins. Only the descendants of Seth, Adam's last son, begotten when Adam was a hundred and thirty years old, knew the great secret. It was communicated to Seth by Adam himself and handed on by Seth to his descendants. The children of Seth were the gnostics.

Seth's seed, the people of gnosis, became objects of the wrath of the Creator-God who tried to drown them in the Flood. Noah, who had agreed to serve the Creator-God "in fear and slavery" was saved from the Flood and the children of Noah have continued to serve the Creator-God ever since.

Not all of the children of Seth were destroyed. A few were saved by the three angels, Abraxas, Sablo and Gamaliel. It is from them that the race of gnostics is descended.

There is enmity between the children of Noah and the children of Seth. The gnostics are the free spirits, the rebels, the People of Truth. The children of Noah are the Believers, slaves to a rigid orthodoxy, who grovel before their god and live in perpetual fear of his displeasure. Whenever they can the children of Noah try to destroy the gnostics. So thoroughly did they wipe out the gnostics in Europe

that, for fifteen gloomy centuries, gnosticism
vanished. (16)

The Alien Man

All gnostics, proto and neo, are outsiders. They do
not feel at ease in the *creatura*. They suspect that
some ghastly error was made by the creator, either
when it produced the cosmos or when it produced
Man. The proto-gnostics felt sure that the whole of
creation was a mistake. One had only to look at the
material world to see that. The gnostic Marcion was
particularly scathing. "Indeed a grand production
and worthy of its God is this world!"

Nothing, in the opinion of the proto-gnostics,
could be more absurd than to imagine that Jesus was
the son of the Creator-God. Nothing could be more
inappropriate than to mix the teachings of Jesus
with those muddled, bloody and often indecent
chronicles of the Jews and their deity. The teachings
of the Old Testament had no place beside the
resplendent gospel of Jesus Christ.

Who or what was Jesus? He was the "Alien Man",
the bringer of the "Call from Without", the
messenger of the God outside Creation. He was sent
to live among the children of Adam, a stranger in a
strange land, to try to awaken them from the sleep
of forgetfulness. Those able to hear the "Call from
Without" were not really a part of the *creatura*.
They were the children of Seth who had never
agreed to serve the Creator-God "in fear and
slavery". They felt lost, exiled in the world of
matter. They were outsiders.

All such could hear the voice of the Alien Man and understand his message. That message, for them, was food for the higher soul, the *pneuma*. It was in the *pneuma*, not in the *psyche*, that the divine spark, *sophia*, was lodged. Possession of the *gnose*, the hidden knowledge, distinguished the gnostics from the mass of men who passed their lives intoxicated with the "wine of forgetfulness". The words of the Alien Man could reawaken in the gnostics the memory of what they had been before they became imprisoned in the material cosmos. They could rise again and return to their former state.

"If a person has the *gnose*, he is a being from on high. If he is called he hears, replies and turns toward Him who calls, in order to ascend to Him... He who thus possesses the *gnose* knows whence he is come and where he is going."

This is from *The Gospel of Truth* attributed to the Alexandrian gnostic, Valentinus. The special knowledge, the *gnosis cardias*, was thus defined by Valentinus.

"What liberates is the knowledge of what we were, what we became; where we were, whereinto we have been thrown; whereto we speed, wherefrom we are redeemed, what birth is and what rebirth... Joy to the man who has rediscovered himself and awakened!"

The Eastern Gnostics

To limit our study of the proto-gnostics to the Western branch of the family would be grossly misleading. There is also an Eastern branch. It is very ancient, going back all the way to the civilization of Harappa and Mohenjo Daro. Its theories regarding the creation were formulated in the Upanishads. Those theories are subtle. Compared with them the speculations of the Alexandrian gnostics seem naive.

"In the beginning"... With these words most creation myths start. They are wrong. There never was a beginning, say the Eastern gnostics. The Supreme Lord, the Ultimate Cause, the indescribable Brahma has no beginning and no end. It simply is. But there is a rhythm, an alternation, similar to the alternation of day and night.

The two phases of this rhythm, the night of Brahma and the day of Brahma, are also called the *nitya* and the *lila*. The *nitya* is unmanifest, the *lila*, the "play of God", is manifest. During the *lila* the Mind Force manifests the entire megalocosmos. That megalocosmos consists of the Cosmic Egg, within which worlds differentiate. *Purusha*, the Cosmic Spirit, (generally thought of as male) gives rise to *prakriti*, Nature, (generally thought of as female). Within *prakriti* all phenomena are produced by the play of three forces (*sattva, rajas, tamas*). The whole process is a play, a manifestation of *maya*, a magical show put on by the Great Magician.

"At the end of a cycle all beings enter into my *prakriti* and at the beginning of a cycle I generate them again.

"Controlling my own *prakriti* I send forth again and again this multitude of beings, helpless under the sway of *maya*." (18)

The *lila*, the play of Brahma, includes the whole megalocosmos with all its galaxies, suns, planets, moons and so on. The sentient beings that arise on planets are only one manifestation of the divine play. The mistake of the Alexandrian gnostics, who represented the Creator-God as an arrogant and basically evil Demiurge, was this. They attributed to the deity the human qualities of good and evil. The Eastern gnostics avoided this error. Brahma is beyond good and evil. The play, the *lila*, will go in accordance with certain laws. The laws are built into the nature of things.

All manifestations proceed in cycles. At the human level there are four phases in the cycle. These are the four *yugas: satya, treta, dvapara* and *kali*. With each succeeding age virtue diminishes and vice increases. This is simply due to the workings of the law of entropy. It does not mean that the Creator-God is either evil or incompetent.

"All actions result from the play of the three forces; only he who is blinded by egoism thinks, 'I am the doer.' "(19)

This is one of the key ideas of the Eastern gnostics. Human beings, like all sentient beings, are bound by action. As long as they are part of the *creatura* they can no more escape from action than they can stop breathing and eating and still remain alive. But certain rare humans, endowed with the *gnosis cardias*, could see through the veil of *maya* and learn to separate themselves from their activities.

They could sit back and watch the play as if they were God himself. In fact they could blend with God for God, the Supreme Brahma, was present in all of his creations. God was the Higher Self, the Atman. Human beings, by freeing themselves from the illusion of separateness, could find that Self within them. Once they had found that Self they would be liberated, able to watch the divine play without bothering to enquire whether it was good or bad, whether it had meaning or no meaning.

Complete liberation from the cycle of births and deaths was possible only for those who had stepped outside the cycle of time with its alternating phases of creation and destruction. Liberation involved stepping out of the *creatura* and entering the *pleroma*, the realm of the imperishable Brahma.

This is certainly no easy undertaking but Yama, King of the Dead, assures us that it can be done and Yama should know, if anyone does.

Arise! Awake! Having attained your boon
now understand it.
As a razor's edge is difficult to pass over
so is the path to the Higher Self difficult to tread.
That Higher Self is not born and does not die:
it sprang from nothing, nothing sprang from it.
Unborn, eternal, everlasting, ancient,
THAT is not killed when the body is killed.
If the slayer thinks he slays, if the slain
thinks he is slain, both are deceived.
THAT slays not nor is it slain.

Smaller than small, greater than great,
in the hearts of all creatures THAT is hidden.
Sitting down it goes far, lying still it goes
everywhere; it is bodiless amid bodies,
changeless amid changes.
How shall an ordinary man understand
THAT to whom both priest and warrior are
as food and death a condiment? (20)

Modern Cosmos, Modern Gnostics

We have outlined the cosmological theories of the proto-gnostics of Alexandria and India. We will now consider the theories of the neo-gnostics.

Let us begin by contrasting the megalocosmos as we envisage it today with the neat little model of the universe that was generally accepted in the second century A.D. The proto-gnostics of Alexandria based their idea of the cosmic prison on this model. Their cosmos consisted of a system of seven concentric crystalline spheres. Each sphere supported a heavenly body. Earth, at the center, was the innermost dungeon of the cosmic prison. Around Earth travelled seven other bodies, Sun, Moon, Mercury, Venus, Mars, Jupiter, Saturn. Beyond these lay the sphere of the fixed stars. Beyond the fixed stars was the empyrean, the realm of the gods.

To the modern-gnostic this model appears merely quaint. He realizes that we dwell in a universe which is enormous in size and constantly expanding.

The Earth, far from being at the center of the stage, is a very minor body in an undistinguished solar system situated in one of the spiral arms of a very ordinary galaxy (the Milky Way). The Milky Way is just one of perhaps a hundred billion galaxies that together constitute the megalocosmos. Every one of these galaxies may contain as many as a hundred billion stars. Many of these stars may have planets. Many of those planets may have generated that system of reversed entropy that we call life.

We have certainly travelled a long way from the simple seven-sphered cosmos of the Alexandrian proto-gnostics.

Nor can the neo-gnostics accept without qualification the idea that a bungling Demiurge created a flawed and essentially evil world purely to satisfy its own will to power. Nature is not that simple.

So what is the world view of the neo-gnostic? It can be formulated more or less as follows.

In the beginning was the Mind Force. The Mind force, working on the surface of those cosmic formations that offered appropriate conditions, created the Life Force which generated living things. Within certain of these living entities the Life Force generated mind. In such beings the Mind Force could become conscious of itself and take charge of its own evolution.

This is the great cycle. Mind passes into matter via life. In certain living organisms mind struggles to take charge of its own destiny. Mind underlies all phenomena but is, at the same time, outside phenomena.

What is the Mind Force?

Let us admit that the Mind Force (the *nous* of the old gnostics) is an invention. It is our own creation, a shadowy replica of our own minds.

How can we justify such an invention?

Very simply. By postulating the Mind Force we compel the universe to make sense.

Is it permissible to compel the universe to make sense?

It is permissible because we have the capacity to do so. We can invent any kind of universe we choose. We cannot know what really exists "out there". The most we can do is to make models, using for our model building the data furnished by our senses. We can extrapolate. We can guess. We ourselves have minds. We are part of the megalocosmos. It produced us and it produced our minds. So the cosmos has mind.

What is mind?

Mind is a force that generates higher levels of order. Can mind exist apart from life? Here the gnostics take a jump into the unknown. Yes, they claim, "mind at large" can and does exist. The primal force, the *logos* that was and is and will be, is the guiding, directing, organizing force throughout the cosmos. It imposes laws. Without it the cosmos would be a chaos in which anything could happen and all would be permitted.

This is the crux of the matter. The cosmos is not a chaos. It is ordered and ordered with the utmost precision. The slightest deviation of certain fundamental constants from their observed values would bring the cosmic drama to a halt. "The universe is a put up job", observed the astronomer Fred Hoyle. It is fine tuned, balanced to an amazing degree, amazing, that is, to those who insist that the whole thing was an accident, a product of a blind chance.

The Mind Force was unmanifested. For reasons beyond our comprehension it became manifested. It took the form of a rapidly expanding megalocosmos. That cosmos was governed from the beginning by a set of forces so delicately balanced that the creative process could and did proceed. In the very first instant after time began the cosmos could either have collapsed into itself or blown up so rapidly that no cosmic concentrations (galaxies, stars, planets, moons) could have formed. It neither collapsed nor did it blow up. It expanded in an orderly fashion, differentiating as it did so. It is still expanding and differentiating, transforming potentials into actualities. It will probably continue to expand and differentiate until all its potentials are actualized. It will then probably contract and return to the unmanifested state.

Mind and Antimind

All the structures in the cosmos depend for their continued existence on the balance between opposing forces. Why do not galaxies collapse into the gigantic black holes that lurk in their centers? Because the spin of the galaxy counterbalances the pull of the black hole. Why do not all the planets fall into the Sun? Because the spin of the solar system counterbalances the Sun's pull. Why does the Sun not collapse in on itself? Because the outward push of its radiation overcomes the pull of gravity.

When the Sun runs out of fuel it will collapse. It will contract into a neutron star. This is the ultimate fate of all stars of this size. The Sun is born, lives, ages, dies. It is now in middle age (about 4.5 billion years old). For another five billion years it is expected to burn quietly and steadily. Then, in its old age, it will expand into a red giant and after that contract into a white dwarf, a dead star slowly cooling in the cosmic vacuum. The human species will perish with it if it does not become extinct long before the death of the Sun.

What should we conclude from this brief survey of cosmic forces? There is no plus without minus. This applies to the Mind Force and to the Life Force. Our model of the cosmos will lack an important element if we fail to take these anti-forces into account.

The cosmic drama results from the interaction of the Force Affirming and the Force Denying, the Mind Force and the Antimind. The Mind Force imposes order, the Antimind creates disorder. The outcome of these interactions depends on a third force that acts like a catalyst. This is the Force Reconciling. The affirming and denying forces would deadlock without the third force and all action would cease. Affirming and denying forces are easy to see but the third force is not.

On the cosmic level the third force provides that element of balance without which the cosmos would either collapse into a black hole or blow up into a tenuous cloud of gas. To generate "interesting objects" and make the cosmic drama possible the original cloud had to clump. The clumps were generated by the action of the third force. They took various forms: galaxies, stars, planets, moons and fragments of matter ranging in size from planetesimals to dust grains. It is on certain of these clumps that sentient beings play their parts.

The Grand Creation

What is the universe? How did it arise? Is it the only universe? Are there other universes, parallel worlds each in its own spacetime framework that interpenetrate with ours but are out of reach of our consciousness?

Perhaps there are such universes. For this reason, because the word *uni*verse implies one and there may be more than one, we use here the word megalocosmos rather than universe. The megalocosmos is defined as that entity which resulted from an explosion, the "big bang", that took place about fifteen billion years ago. At this point our spacetime began.

Why did it start?

Because the Mind Force chose to change from the unmanifested to the manifested state.

How do we know?

We don't. We guess. The point is that it did start. Spacetime had a beginning. The megalocosmos has not always existed. The curtain rose on the cosmic drama. The play began.

How?

The theoretical physicists have had a fine time struggling to answer this question. Here, very briefly, is the model they have constructed.

The seed from which the megalocosmos grew appeared at "Planck time". Why Planck time? Because time itself is quantized. Time is not infinitely divisible. Planck time (10^{-43} seconds) is the shortest interval of time that can exist.

So what happened at Planck time?

Something emerged. From what did it emerge? And what was the something?

The gnostic would say that the Mind Force (*nous*) created Thought (*ennoia*). The material world is a manifestation of *ennoia*. The physicist would say that the quantum vacuum that existed before time acquired a prodigious amount of negative energy. This negative energy took the form of a repulsive force, an antigravity. So powerful was the inflationary force that the seed of the budding megalocosmos doubled in size every 10^{-34} seconds. The entity that did the doubling was devoid of matter and of radiation. It was a "no thing", a "false vacuum". But the grand repulsion caused that "no thing" to grow in volume from one thousandth millionth of the size of a proton to the diameter of a tennis ball. This was the "big bang".

All this happened in a minute fraction of a second. Alan Guth of M.I.T. who invented the grand inflation assures us that it began working at 10^{-35} seconds and stopped at 10^{-32} seconds. This is just as well. Had the expansion continued at this rate the megalocosmos would have virtually evaporated. Neither radiation nor matter would have formed within it.

But why did the grand inflation start and what caused it to stop? What became of antigravity? Why does it not manifest today?

Difficult questions!

The truth is that we cannot be sure that antigravity ever existed. Antigravity is mind created. It is a thought in the minds of theoretical physicists. They find it necessary to explain the universal expansion. At some point or other the universe exploded and the results of this explosion are still with us. The galaxies are rapidly receding from one another. The fabric of spacetime inflates with every day that passes. The whole megalocosmos is blowing up like a gigantic balloon. What started the expansion? Antigravity.

Perhaps. It is hard to argue about an event that occupied only a fraction of a picosecond and took place about fifteen billion years ago. Though they may theorize at length on the subject of the instant of creation it still presents a puzzle to the physicists. A *something* emerged from a *nothing*, breaking the laws of the conservation of energy and matter expressed in the term *nihil ex nihilo*. Nothing from nothing.

"The inflationary universe attempts to build the universe from *almost* nothing. In fact the universe may be the ultimate free lunch." (21)

The emergence of something out of nothing is a tough idea to swallow. Does it not sound like a miracle, an exercise of free will by some all powerful deity?

"And the earth was without form, and void; and darkness was upon the face of the deep. And the spirit of God moved on the face of the waters.

"And God said, Let there be light: and there was light." (22)

There was light indeed! At 10^{-32} seconds the swelling fabric of spacetime was flooded with heat. Its temperature was 10^{27} degrees Kelvin. *That is hot.* The surface temperature of a very hot star giving off 100,000 times as much radiation as does our Sun is only 3×10^4 degrees Kelvin. So the heat of the new born universe was about a billion, billion, billion times hotter than the hottest star. God created light with a vengeance! Where did all that energy come from? No one knows.

God and the Physicists

And no one can know!

The models which the theoretical physicists offer to explain what happened at the moment of creation are all mind-created. True they are expressed in very abstruse mathematical equations but the equations are also mind-created. They represent a way of depicting the interaction of forces, like the familiar equation $E=mc^2$ which expresses the relationship of energy to matter.

The physicists have struggled mightily to generate a model of the emerging universe which would eliminate the need for a Creator-God. Physicists are understandably nervous about God. God does not fit into their equations. God is presumably a force, but an unpredictable force. You can never tell what

God will do next. Even Einstein, who seemed to
know what God was up to ("God does not play
dice,") had to admit that the deity was a puzzle.

Just how free was God? Did God have to play the
game according to the rules? If so, who or what
made the rules? Is God a prisoner of His own laws? Is
it true, as the old story asserts, that "even the Lord
God cannot beat the ace with the deuce"? (23)

Einstein was a gnostic and a deeply religious man.
"Religion without science is blind. Science without
religion is lame." Einstein's God was "the Old One",
subtle, elusive, hard to approach. "Quantum
mechanics is very impressive," he wrote in a letter to
Max Born, "but an inner voice tells me that it is not
the real thing. The theory produces a good deal but
it hardly brings us closer to the secret of the Old
One. I am, at all events, convinced that He does not
play dice." (24)

Einstein's "inner voice" was the *gnosis cardias*, the
"knowledge of the heart".

But if God does not play dice what sort of game
does he play? Is God free to break the rules? "What
I'm really interested in is whether God could have
made the world in a different way, that is whether
the necessity for logical simplicity leaves any
freedom at all."

Einstein concluded that God could not create a
universe that was not logically consistent, a view he
expressed in a very gnostic aphorism. "Subtle is the
Lord, but malicious He is not." He explained the
statement by adding that "Nature hides its secret
because of its essential loftiness, but not by means of
ruse". Nature plays fair.

Well, perhaps. But who or what is Nature?

The gnostic answers this question by saying that Nature is the Mind Force which generated the Life Force which in turn regenerated mind. In certain living entities, of which Man is an example, ordinary mind has the possibility of being transformed into higher mind (*buddhi*) which blends with the Mind Force, thus completing the cycle of creation.

Why has the Mind Force eluded the physicists whose job it is to define the forces which shape our world? The reason is simple. The Mind Force cannot be measured by any instrument available even in the most perfectly equipped physics laboratory. That which cannot be measured cannot be expressed in equations. As physicists think entirely in terms of equations they cannot fit either the Mind Force or the Life Force into their scheme of things.

SIX FORCES OF THE MEGALOCOSMOS

Forces Measurable	Forces Unmeasurable
Strong Force	Mind Force
Weak Force	Life Force
Electro-magnetic	
Gravitation	

But how do we know the Mind Force exists?

To the modern gnostic the answer to this question seems obvious. Open your eyes and see, look within yourself, look about you! Are you not surrounded by the products of the Life Force in the form of countless living organisms ranging in size from bacteria to whales? Do you not detect in these organisms the workings of mind, a mind which, in some respects, is cleverer than your own? Are not you yourself the possessor of a mind and a part of the human collective mind, a formidable affair that has accumulated skills and information over thousands of years? And is there not evidence that the human mind, defective though it is in many respects, can be strengthened, freed of its illusions, enlightened, purified? Is it not clear, moreover, that this process of self-transformation, which involves not only the intellect but other functions as well, is the proper work of Man?

"The more the universe seems comprehensible, the more it seems pointless." (25) This from Stephen Weinberg, theoretical physicist and Nobel Laureate. Sure it seems pointless if one insists on ignoring the higher forces. Gravity, the strong force, the electromagnetic and the weak force are no doubt manifestations of the superforce which weaves together spacetime and matter. But let us not rule out the existence of other forces merely because we lack the instruments with which to measure these forces. The Mind Force works within us. To deny its existence is to deny the highest aspect of our own being. The physicists may have discovered, or perhaps they have invented, that mysterious entity they call the superforce. But it was the Mind Force that invented the physicists!

A Working Universe

So what happened next, after the big bang?

The budding megalocosmos exploded again!

Really those early stages of cosmos formation were incredibly violent. First came the big bang, then came the little bang. It was really not so little either. What caused it? Matter met antimatter. When matter meets antimatter there is an explosion. They annihilate each other in a flash of gamma rays.

Where did the matter come from? It came from quarks.

What are quarks? They are thoughts, physicists' thoughts. No one has ever seen a quark. But presumably they exist. Murray Gell-Mann got the Nobel Award for thinking of quarks. "Three quarks for Muster Marks." This from *Finnegans Wake*. Was James Joyce the possessor of the gift of prophecy or a theoretical physicist without realizing it?

Anyway there were quarks, wild quarks, dashing about in the incredibly hot proto-universe. They did not dash about for long. At 10^{-6} seconds they were tamed, corralled by the strong force in groups of three to make protons and neutrons in which they have been locked ever since.

The universe was shaping up. Matter was forming out of radiation. $m = E/c^2$. Which means that it takes an awful lot of energy to make one unit of matter. But there was one snag. Whenever matter is generated an equal amount of antimatter is also generated. When matter meets antimatter they annihilate each other. One is left with nothing but gamma rays.

Back to square one.

How can one ever get a megalocosmos started if
the matter and antimatter keep destroying one
another? Separate the two? Make two
megalocosmoses, one of matter, the other of
antimatter? It is possible, but what would do the
separating? The Mind Force? Perhaps. But the
physicists prefer a different theory. Let Paul Davies
explain. (26) There is GUT, the Grand Unified
Theory, and GUT suggests that, at the critical
moment when matter took the form of protons and
neutrons, there were exactly a billion and one
particles of matter for every billion particles of
antimatter. So a billion protons destroyed a billion
antiprotons leaving one proton over.

One proton in every billion! And out of this poor
residue we must make a megalocosmos containing at
least a hundred billion galaxies each containing
about a hundred billion stars. Surely you must be
joking, Dr. Davies!

But Paul Davies, as these clever physicists will,
takes refuge from arguments in the mathematics of
GUT which are abstruse and beyond the reach of
less well endowed minds. Besides, he points out, the
radiation of the little bang can be calculated. It is
still around, as is the radiation from the big bang,
very much diluted of course by the expansion of the
universe. But there it is. The cosmic energy books
balance nicely.

So now we have enough matter free of antimatter
to build a megalocosmos. It took three hundred
thousand years for the expanding megalocosmos to
cool down enough for matter as we know it to form.
The free electrons which had been buzzing about all

over the place were snared by the electric force and linked to protons to form hydrogen atoms. The rest were snared by helium nuclei. With the free electrons trapped in atoms the cosmic fog cleared. For the first time since the creation light could pass freely through the megalocosmos. (27)

What was the megalocosmos at that time? It was a gas cloud, 90% hydrogen, 10% helium. But how does one manage to build a cosmic drama full of heroes, villains and other interesting characters out of a cloud of hot hydrogen and helium?

Impossible!

But not any more impossible than creating a megalocosmos out of nothing. In any case the Mind Force solved the problem. It imposed on the gas cloud a higher level of order. As a result the gas cloud clumped. The first clumps formed 12,500 million years ago and were enormous. Each contained enough matter to form a hundred billion stars. They spun like gigantic pinwheels. They had to if they were not to collapse into the enormous black holes that formed in their centers. Their spiral arms spread far into space. They were the primordial galaxies, squeezed close together in those early days. Later, as spacetime expanded, they spread further and further apart.

Second order clumps formed within the galaxies. These were the earliest stars made of hydrogen and helium. There was nothing else from which they could be made. The stars were alchemical factories, transformers of matter. As they contracted under the influence of gravity the hydrogen in their cores was compressed and heated. At a temperature of two hundred million degrees the protons of the hydrogen atoms collided with enough energy to fuse. They formed helium nuclei and the energy given off in the process further heated the star.

The transformation of hydrogen into helium was only a beginning. Stars varied greatly in size. The larger the star the hotter it gets and the more rapidly it consumes its fuel. The short lives of very large stars terminate in prodigious explosions. They become supernovas. For a short period they generate as much radiant energy as the entire galaxy of which they are part. The explosion scatters into space a huge dust cloud and in that cloud, formed during the last few seconds of the star's life, are all the elements of the Periodic Table, including the 24 needed for life.

It was from the dust generated by such exploding stars that our solar system was formed. It condensed some 4.5 billion years ago, taking the form of a flattened dust cloud spinning about a center that gradually sucked into itself nearly all the contents of the cloud. This central mass contracted and heated. After about ten million years it became dense enough and hot enough for fusion reactions to begin.

So the Sun was born, a medium sized star that burned quietly and steadily transforming matter, mainly hydrogen, into heavier elements and radiation. The Sun is a well behaved star. Its output of radiation does not fluctuate much. This is just as well. Life on Earth could not exist if the Sun developed a habit of flaring up from time to time.

Planets and Life

Now we are coming close to home. We have a solar system. We have a star, a modest and well behaved luminary. We have seven planets rotating at different distances around the star of which the four inner (Mercury, Venus, Earth, Mars) are rocky and the rest, from Jupiter out, are gaseous and consist chiefly of hydrogen. Though the inner planets contain all the elements needed for life it seems to have arisen only on one of them. That planet is Earth.

So how did life on Earth begin? Did it come from outside? Was it generated *de novo* on our planet?

Let us go back to Earth's beginnings. Four thousand four hundred and fifty million years ago the planet Earth was more or less complete. It was hot. Its atmosphere was composed of a mixture of carbon dioxide, ammonia, methane and steam. Its oceans were starting to form. They boiled. The atmosphere crackled. Huge electrical storms raged and sparkled. In those powerful electrical discharges a wealth of chemicals was made, amino acids, nucleic acids, all the building blocks needed for life. Deluges of scalding rain carried down with them the chemical products of the electric storms. The primordial seas attained the consistency of hot soup. In addition to being hot they were highly radioactive, for many radioactive elements, now decayed, were still emitting particles in those early days.

In short the young planet Earth was a very lively chemical laboratory in the oceans of which all sorts of chemical combinations were taking place. We can be reasonably sure that on Earth's sister planet, Venus, similar reactions were occurring as they were, no doubt, on Earth's other neighbor, Mars. But Venus, circling 70 million miles from the Sun, proved a bit too hot for living things. Mars, 137 million miles from the Sun, was a bit too cold. Only the Earth, 93 million miles from the Sun, provided just the right conditions for the drama of organic evolution.

So the show began. How? We cannot answer this question with any certainty. There are those, Francis Crick among them, who take the view that life on Earth was "seeded" from outside, brought in on a rocket in the form of dried bacteria.

Who sent out that rocket more than three billion years ago? Intelligent beings on another planet whose doom was sealed by the imminent death of their star. They wanted life to spread and evolve and knew that bacteria (if freeze dried) could survive long trips. So they sent bacteria to our young planet. Life on Earth started at the bacterial level. This is the theory of Directed Panspermia. (28)

But how did life begin on that hypothetical planet whose intelligent beings sent the rocket? Directed Panspermia merely transfers the problem of the origin of life to another planet.

So how *did* life get started?

What Is Life?

Life as we know it is a self-reproducing system of three macromolecules, DNA (deoxyribonucleic acid), RNA (ribonucleic acid), and protein. This is life's "holy trinity". DNA carries the basic code. Its giant molecules consist of strings of organic bases labelled A.T.G.C. (for adenine, thymine, guanine, cytosine). DNA is translated into the language of RNA which also has four bases with U. (uracil) in the place of T. RNA provides the template on which proteins (made up of strings of twenty amino acids) are put together. Protein, in the form of special enzymes, synthesizes both DNA and RNA.

All three are interdependent. No protein without RNA. No RNA without DNA. No DNA or RNA without protein.

Which came first? We don't know. The modern gnostic maintains that the Mind Force generated the Life Force. The Life Force produced the morphogenetic field (29) that brought the three components of life's holy trinity together in such a way that they constituted the simplest possible living organism.

What is the simplest possible living organism? It is a microscopic globule containing DNA, RNA and protein, enclosed in some sort of membrane. It might be called the primitive naked protoplast. Starting with these globules of protoplasm the Life Force proceeded to play variations on the original theme. The variations became increasingly complex. New and ever more elaborate morphogenetic fields were evolved and new holons (30) emerged having properties not possessed by the entities from which they had arisen.

The great tree of life began to grow, very slowly at first then more and more rapidly. (See diagram on following page.) Each level of growth was marked

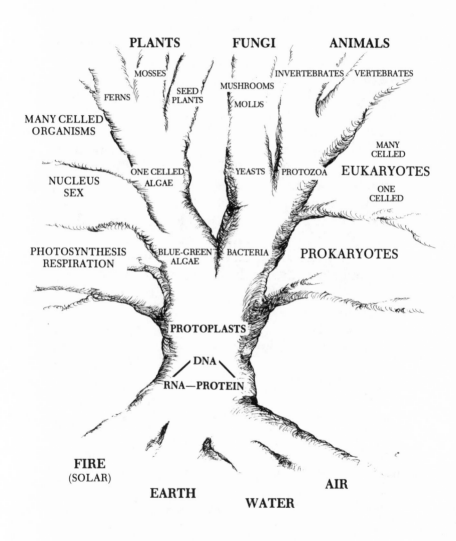

BRANCHES OF THE TREE OF LIFE

by the emergence of a new invention by the Life Force, a new and higher level of order. The seven major developments of the tree of life were as follows.

I. Protoplasts. These were the simplest possible living things, mere globules of DNA, RNA and protein. They floated in billions in the primordial soup and used the materials in the soup to generate more globules.

II. Bacteria. These entities were more highly organized than the protoplasts, but still very small. They too swarmed in billions in the primitive seas and used up the soup at such a rate that they were in danger of eating themselves out of existence.

III. Blue-green algae. These entities were one of the most brilliant inventions of the Life Force. In them the Force developed the biochemical mechanism that underlies almost all the food chains in Earth's biosphere. This mechanism was photosynthesis. Instead of feeding on organic molecules randomly formed in the primordial soup these blue-green algae drew their energy directly from the Sun. Using this energy they were able to synthesize all the complex organic molecules needed for their existence from such simple substances as carbon dioxide, water, nitrates and a variety of minerals. They were *autotrophs*, self-feeders. From them arose the vast array of green plants on which the entire animal kingdom depends for its food.

IV. Respiration. The invention of photosynthesis had one very important consequence. It poured into Earth's atmosphere a powerful poison. This poison was oxygen.

Those accustomed to thinking of oxygen as the breath of life, (which it is for us and for most living things) may be surprised to find it described as a poison. But poisonous it was to the billions of bacteria that swarmed in the primitive seas. The bacteria were what is known as anaerobes. They generated their energy by the process of anaerobic fermentation. A lot of bacteria still do this, including some very bad characters such as the organisms that produce tetanus and gas gangrene.

So the Life Force came up with another brilliant invention. It devised the *mitochondria*. These organelles were developed from certain photosynthetic purple bacteria that had learned how to handle oxygen. They were incorporated into the cells of both plants and animals. They enabled the organisms possessing them to use oxygen to burn their fuel in a regulated manner by a process called respiration. Both plants and animals respire, taking in oxygen and giving off carbon dioxide. The energy of the Sun that is locked into organic molecules by photosynthesis is released from those molecules by respiration. What becomes of the energy? It is taken up by a special molecule called ATP (adenosine triphosphate) which is one of the key molecules of life. It supplies the energy needed for almost all the chemical transactions of the cell.

V. The Nucleus. In bacteria and in blue-green algae the DNA carrying the genetic code slops around loose in the cell. It takes the form of a single long thread which splits lengthwise when the cell divides. This is effective for simple forms which do not carry much genetic information. In more complex forms that carry far more genetic information the single thread of DNA would become impossibly long.

So the Life Force generated another holon, the nucleated cell, in which the DNA was organized in a group of short, neat packets called chromosomes. When the cells of such organisms are about to divide, the chromosomes parade in the center of the cell, each splits down the middle, each half of the chromosome is dragged off in the opposite direction by a special mechanism called the spindle. Each daughter cell gets a complete new set of chromosomes. This process is called *mitosis*.

Organisms possessing nucleated cells are called *eukaryotes*. The more primitive cells without nuclei (bacteria and blue-green algae) are called *prokaryotes*.

VI. Sex. What is sex? Why did the Life Force invent it?

Sex provides a method of mixing genes which commonly come in two forms, dominant and recessive (labelled A and a, B and b and so on). As chromosomes are paired a given individual can have a gene in the form AA (double dominant), Aa (heterozygous), or aa (double recessive). Almost all the cells in our bodies have such paired genes, one from father, one from mother. This is called the *diploid* condition.

The exceptions are the sex cells. These cells result from what is called reduction division (*meiosis*) which separates the members of each pair of chromosomes. As a result each pair of genes is also separated. In us humans our diploid cells have 46 chromosomes but our sex cells, produced by reduction division, have only 23. This is the *haploid* condition.

The sex cells (gametes) come in two forms, large immobile ova carried by the female, small mobile sperms produced by the male. A new life begins when the nucleus of the sperm fuses with the nucleus of the egg. The cell which results is called a zygote. In the zygote the two forms of each gene will be reblended. Depending on the makeup of the parents the zygote may have AA, aa or Aa.

Such is the process of genetic segregation and reblending that underlies sexual reproduction. It is surely one of the most extraordinary inventions of the Life Force!

To bring sperms and ova together the Life Force generated the sex organs and the sexual instincts. The ingenuity and variety displayed in these organs and instincts cannot fail to arouse the admiration of anyone but the most hardened neo-Darwinian. (31)

So in the plant world we see flowers of great complexity and variety. They are devised entirely to bribe various insects which, for a drink of nectar or some other satisfaction, transfer the male cells (pollen) to the receptive female organ (the stigma). Flowers are completely unnecessary. A highly successful family of plants, the grasses, manages without them, relying entirely on the wind to transfer pollen. In spite of this the Life Force invented flowers expending on some of these organs, particularly in the orchid family, an extraordinary amount of ingenuity. Why? From a strictly Darwinian standpoint flowers would seem a needless extravagance. Evidently the Life Force has no use for Darwin or Darwinism. The Life Force is an artist.

In the animal kingdom the devices used to bring together sperms and eggs are no less extraordinary. The usual method of transfer involves an intromittent organ (penis) that injects the sperm into the female body. But this method is reversed in the sea horse in which the female introduces her eggs into the body of the male who rears the young. The octopus detaches one of its arms and sends it off to find the female if it can (a swimming penis). And why, in the name of all the love gods, has the Life Force equipped the male flea with the longest and most complicated penis (in relation to the animal's size) of all the creatures in the animal kingdom?

VII. Multicellular Organisms. For about 1.5 billion years the Life Force was satisfied with one-celled organisms. There were one-celled plants (algae) and one-celled animals (protozoa). In them the Life Force incorporated all the foregoing inventions. These single-celled organisms photosynthesized, they respired, they had sex. They managed very well and there seemed absolutely no reason for the Life Force to invent anything more complicated.

But the Life Force had a program and that program involved the genesis of a creature in which the original Mind Force could become conscious of itself. One-celled animals were too simple. Multicellular creatures were called for. The switch was quite abrupt. Suddenly, judged by the geological time scale, multicellular creatures

appeared in the oceans. This happened about 1300
million years ago, first among the plants, later
among the animals.

Gaia

By the Cambrian period the oceans swarmed with
complex forms, trilobites, ammonites, crinoids,
various seaweeds. The Great Life Plan unfolded
with increasing rapidity. The two major animal
groups, vertebrates and invertebrates, emerged by
the Ordovician, 500 million years ago. In the animal
world nine major themes emerged and were played
on by the Life Force with many variations. These
forms are presently exemplified by starfish, worms,
slugs, insects, reptiles, amphibia, birds and
mammals. Members of both the plant and animal
kingdoms emerged from the oceans and invaded the
dry land which, in those early days, consisted of a
single super-continent.

The drama of life was violently affected by wild
fluctuations in Earth's climate. Bitter ice ages
alternated with spells of steamy tropical warmth.
From time to time the whole planet was shaken by
cosmic catastrophes that nearly brought the whole
drama of life to a halt. One of these, the Permian
terminal catastrophe, resulted in the destruction of
96% of all species of marine animals. This happened
about 245 million years ago and probably resulted
from a head on collision of the planet Earth with a
comet.

There were plenty of other catastrophes,
including one at the end of the Cretaceous period

which appears to have wiped out the last of the dinosaurs, leaving the stage clear for the emergence of the mammals. It was caused by a collision of our planet with a giant meteorite.

It seems surprising that the Great Life Plan has continued and unfolded for about 400 million years. Again and again it was almost brought to a halt not only by cosmic collisions but also by climatic variations and changes in the planet's overall chemistry. The spaceship Earth could easily have gone the way of its sister ship Venus, which has proved a total failure as far as the Life Force is concerned. Venus has a dense atmosphere of carbon dioxide mixed with droplets of sulfuric acid and its surface temperature is hot enough to melt lead. How did Earth escape a similar fate?

To answer this question we must refer to the Gaia Hypothesis formulated by James Lovelock and hailed by Stewart Brand as "one of the epochal insights of this century". The Gaia Hypothesis proposes that "the entire life of Earth, through its atmosphere and ocean, functions effectively as one self-regulating organism: Gaia." (32)

To understand how delicately balanced this regulatory mechanism is we need only consider the concentration of two gases in Earth's atmosphere. These gases are oxygen and carbon dioxide. Both gases are absolutely necessary for life as it now exists on Earth. Without oxygen all those creatures, plant and animal, that generate their energy through respiration would perish. Without carbon dioxide the process of photosynthesis, on which animals,

fungi and bacteria depend for their food, would
come to a halt.

Now consider the exquisite balance that Gaia (the
Greek goddess of the Earth) maintains between
these two gases. The oxygen content of the
atmosphere is held at 21%. This concentration of
the gas enables us not only to breathe freely but also
to start fires. But an increase of only 4% in the
concentration of oxygen in the air would render fires
deadly. Any forest fire started by a lightning flash in
25% oxygen would burn so fiercely that all the
forests on Earth would soon be consumed.

Now consider the concentration of carbon
dioxide. There is only 0.03% of this gas in our
atmosphere. It is something of a miracle that, with
so little carbon dioxide to work with, green plants
manage to generate enough organic matter to keep
the biosphere going. But carbon dioxide is a
potentially dangerous gas. It has a way of trapping
the heat radiation of the Sun, thereby raising the
temperature of a planet (the greenhouse effect).
Lovelock has calculated that, without the influence
of life, the Earth's atmosphere would contain 98%
of carbon dioxide and its temperature would be a
searing 290 degrees Celsius (554 degrees F.) The
temperature on the surface of Venus, which also has
98% carbon dioxide in its atmosphere, is 477
degrees C. (Lead melts at 327 degrees C.)

How does Gaia manage to keep the carbon
dioxide levels down in the Earth's atmosphere?
Plants, during the hours of daylight, fix a lot of the
gas by means of photosynthesis. But during the
hours of darkness plants respire and respiration puts

carbon dioxide back into the atmosphere. It would seem that Gaia takes most of the carbon dioxide out of circulation either by dissolving it in the oceans or by locking it up in carbonates. Most of the carbon dioxide on Earth is so locked up. There are entire mountain ranges made out of calcium carbonate in the form of dolomite, marble, limestone, or chalk. A good deal of carbon is locked up in the form of deposits of coal and oil, now being poured back into the atmosphere as carbon dioxide by foolish humans who do not know what they are doing.

Could the aforesaid foolish humans wreck Gaia's balancing act and set off processes that would doom the whole biosphere? Lovelock thinks that they could. He has even invented a scientist to do the job, a Dr. Intensli Eeger who, by his well-intentioned meddling, manages to wreck Gaia's feedback mechanisms, thus transforming the Earth into a barren planet.

Lovelock is prepared to accept the idea that *Homo sapiens*, with its huge collective intelligence, might be regarded as the Gaian nervous system, with a brain that can consciously anticipate environmental changes.(33) But let us not fool ourselves. In our present muddled state we are not so much the nervous system of Gaia as a malignant growth, busily destroying the foundations on which our own life support systems rest. Something seems to have gone seriously wrong.

What Went Wrong?

Here we are, all five billion of us. Three and a half billion years of evolution were needed to produce us, a relatively hairless ape that is clever enough to journey to the moon but not wise enough to prevent itself from damaging its own planet. What sort of creature is this being that has the effrontery to call itself *Homo sapiens sapiens*? (34) Here is one view expressed by that enlightened monarch, the King of the Brobdingnanians.

"I cannot but conclude the bulk of your natives to be the most pernicious race of little odious vermin that Nature ever suffered to crawl on the surface of the earth." (35)

Exaggerated? Perhaps. But not by much. If you doubt this, study the history of the twentieth century. Somewhere along the line of evolution between *Homo erectus* and *Homo sapiens* something appears to have gone terribly wrong. So two important questions demand an answer.

What went wrong?

Can we put it right?

In this chapter we will seek an answer to the first question. In the next part of the book we will seek an answer to the second.

So what went wrong?

Gurdjieff had an answer. He propounded it in *Beelzebub's Tales to His Grandson*. (36) It was the fault of a certain Sacred Individual who failed to calculate correctly the paths of the planet Earth and the comet Kondoor. As a result of this miscalculation the planet and comet collided and two large fragments were knocked off the planet.

These two fragments, the Moon and Anulios, had to be nourished somehow lest the Harmony- of-Reciprocal-Maintenance-of-All-Cosmic-Concen- trations be upset. So it was decided by a Most High Commission of Sacred Individuals that certain two legged beings on the planet Earth should, by their existence, maintain the detached fragments of their planet. It was also foreseen that, should those three-brained beings ever learn the true cause of their inner slavery, they would be unwilling to continue their existence and would destroy themselves.

To prevent this occurrence the Chief-Common- Universal-Arch-Chemist-Physicist Angel Looisos caused a certain "something" to grow at the base of the spines of these three-brained beings. That something was called the organ kundabuffer. Among its properties was one which made certain that the three-brained beings should "perceive reality topsy turvey". As a result they would never understand the real cause of their inner slavery.

Although the organ kundabuffer was later destroyed by that same Arch-Chemist-Physicist Looisos, its properties had by then become crystallized in the common presences of the human population of the Earth. These crystallized properties of the organ kundabuffer had two effects. First, they caused the human inhabitants of the planet to increase their numbers very rapidly. Second, they caused them to behave in a manner never before observed among three-brained beings of other planets, namely that they would suddenly, without rhyme or reason, begin destroying one another's existence.

This rather elaborate Gurdjieffian allegory places the blame for Man's peculiar behavior on the "almost criminal unforeseeingness" of certain Sacred Individuals who were in charge of traffic in this solar system.

But what, we may ask, was that maleficent organ kundabuffer? And how, if it was destroyed, did it continue to exert its baneful effect on Man's psyche? A search for answers to these questions could lead us further and further into that jungle of allegory with which Gurdjieff surrounded his ideas. Rather than risk getting lost in that jungle I propose to place before the reader another theory, solidly based on the findings of modern neuroanatomy and physiology.

Here, in brief, is the answer to the question, "What went wrong?".

The early hominid, *Homo erectus*, from which we appear to be descended, had a brain volume of about 600 cc. It appears that *erectus* underwent a whole series of mutations about 500,000 years ago. These mutations, which probably included reduction of body hair, chiefly took the form of a great enlargement of the cranium and a corresponding expansion of the roof brain within that cranium. The result was a new breed of hominid, *Homo sapiens*, with an average brain volume of 1400 c.c.

It was this sudden enlargement of the neocortex that created difficulties for *Homo sapiens*. "In creating the human brain nature has wildly overshot the mark," (this from Arthur Koestler whose book, *The Ghost in the Machine*, (37) should be read by anyone interested in understanding what went wrong).

His large new brain at first did little to improve the lot of its owner. That powerful biocomputer, capable of generating the symphonies of Beethoven, the sonnets of Shakespeare, the equations of Special and General Relativity, the Gospels, the Upanishads, and the Gothic cathedrals, came without an instruction manual. The poor savage who had received this "unsolicited gift" used it at first only to make rather elegant stone tools and to decorate the walls of his caves with very creditable representations of various animals. It was not until the end of the Neolithic Age that humans quite suddenly began to learn how to use their big brains. The result was a string of inventions (agriculture, animal husbandry, irrigation, pottery, weaving, boat-building, house-building) that laid the foundations of what we call civilization.

Unfortunately the expansion of the new brain was not accompanied by a corresponding refinement of the old brains. These brains lie beneath the new brain and generate the instincts and emotions. Having no spoken language they are out of touch with the roof brain. They produce affects, the primitive urges, sex, hunger, fear, hatred and so on, that sweep away reason and take charge of the whole machine.

That perceptive neurophysiologist, Paul MacLean, has compared us humans to a trio consisting of a man, a horse and a crocodile. The

man cannot talk to the horse or the crocodile
because they have no spoken language. But both
beasts are very powerful. They are liable, in crises,
to take charge. As they have no capacity for
reasoning their behavior is often disastrously
inappropriate, especially in the crowded, dangerous
world that we moderns have built. It is the horse
and the crocodile that have, between them, made
such an unholy mess of our history. Unless these
beasts can be brought under the control of the
reason they may lead *Homo sapiens* down the road
to extinction.

Our elaborate new intellectual brains do not work
very well either. They have developed a disastrous
habit of generating fantasies and these fantasies cut
us off from the real world. *We are the only animal
on Earth that consistently lies to itself.* Many
animals practice deception to confuse their enemies
and such deceptions have survival value. But man
lies to *himself* and his habit of self-deception has no
survival value whatever. It cuts him off from the
real world and causes him to inhabit a world of
dreams. It fills his awareness with paranoid
delusions which cause him to squander his collective
brain power on inventing destructive devices instead
of using it to solve the urgent problems he confronts.
If the destructive devices are ever used they may
prove fatal, not only to Man but also to the whole of
Earth's biosphere.

Here then is a scientific answer to the question,
"What went wrong?". Man is the victim of an
evolutionary error, an error in brain building.
Nature or the Mind Force was in too much of a

hurry. It created our truly magnificent neocortex without setting up a clear chain of command to ensure that the new brain, seat of the reason, would dominate the old brains, seats of the instincts and emotions. The result was a highly suggestible, unstable naked ape that lived largely in the world of fantasy, was full of paranoid delusions and chronically liable to panic.

When in danger or in doubt
Run in circles, scream and shout.

Arthur Koestler, that gloomy Hungarian, was not at all pleased with our creator. "Nature has let us down, God seems to have left the receiver off the hook, and time is running out." Of course there is nothing to prevent us from finding fault with God, Nature, the Mind Force, the Life Force or whatever we choose to call the power that formed us. But what good does it do? The fossil record suggests that Nature is cruel, wasteful, careless and seemingly quite indifferent as to the outcome of her experiments. Ninety-nine percent of all the species that have ever existed are now extinct. It was this carelessness of Nature that so shocked the Victorian poet.

Are God and Nature then at strife
That Nature lends such evil dream
So careful of the type she seems
So careless of the single life:
So careful of the type? but no.

From scarped cliff and quarried stone
She cries, "A thousand types are gone:
I care for nothing, all shall go.

(Alfred Tennyson, "In Memoriam")

Tennyson's lament is entirely justified. We would
be fools indeed to portray the Life Force or Nature
as a loving mother passionately concerned with the
fate of her children. If we want to whine and
complain and accuse her of unfairness we are
perfectly at liberty to do so. The trouble is that it
won't help. Nature, if one can coax an answer out of
her, would reply to our complaints more or less as
follows.

"It is true that you are a sorry lot, unbalanced,
hysterical, half-completed creatures with a
tendency to go mad *en masse* and a habit of thinking
of yourselves as the Lords of Creation. But you are
not the lords of anything. You are slaves. You like
your slavery. You would rather be slaves than free.
But why find fault with me? If I left you incomplete
it was to see if you could complete yourselves. I gave
you the power to carry out this work of self-
completion. Stop complaining and do it or I'll throw
you out and put something else in your place!"

There speaks Old Mother Hardass. No
sentimentality about Nature! Certainly things have
not been made easy for us. The attitude of our
creator toward us seems to be wildly inconsistent.
The Great Work of self-completion is said to be
against Nature and against God, and that with good
reason. That work has been made terribly difficult.

We might justifiably conclude that Nature does not want us to discover the great secret.

But Nature has two aspects, as previously noted. There is no plus without minus. So, on the one hand, Nature blinds us, deceives us, keeps us enslaved, and on the other she seems to encourage us to become liberated. No wonder we feel confused!

One thing is certain. Those who have discovered the great secret must use it. We now know what went wrong. Next we must seek an answer to the question, "How can we put it right?".

II

THE FANTASY WORK

Slaves and Masters

What is the Work?

It can be defined very simply.

The Work involves the transformation of a muddled, delusion-ridden slave into an enlightened, integrated master.

Let us define what we mean by the words master and slave.

The slave has no control over his or her life, is pushed about by external forces, is at the mercy of casual impressions, a slave to habits, most of them bad, a prey to credulity, suggestibility, hopes and fears.

Above all the slave is a creature of fantasy. It inhabits a world of dreams. It is cut off from knowledge of the real world by a mechanism in its brain, the working of which generates delusions. The slave lies to itself about itself and about everything else. It does not know that it lies. It is a slave that dreams that it is free. It is a liar that dreams that it knows the truth.

The master has liberated himself from the delusion-producing mechanism in his brain. He is a dweller in the real world. In order to enter this world he has had to sacrifice his dreams. He has dared to confront the truth about himself and about his fellow men. He has been strong enough and cunning enough to escape from the prison in which the slaves pass their lives. He is fully awake. He has seen the truth and the truth has set him free. But he has paid a mighty high price to attain that freedom.

Think very carefully. Can you pay that price? Do you dare to confront reality? Can you bear to know the truth about yourself and your fellow humans?

That truth is not in the least bit comforting. Here we have several thousand millions of human beings going round like blindfolded donkeys in a treadmill, driven from behind by the stick of fear, lured forward from in front by the carrot of greed. The overseer of the Treadmill, a great and terrible spirit, has made certain that the donkeys do not try to escape. The spirit has done this by the very simple procedure of hypnotizing the donkeys into thinking that they are already free.

Can the paralysing grip of this hypnosis be relaxed?

For most of the donkeys it cannot. Any well-meaning liberator who attempts to awaken them from their state of sleep will certainly be attacked, kicked and bitten, for daring to suggest to the donkeys that they are slaves. Such a suggestion robs them of their fondest illusion, the illusion that they are free and the masters of their fate. The donkeys much prefer to live in their unreal world. It is easy to dream, hard to confront reality. Given a choice between what is easy and what is difficult, the donkeys will inevitably follow the easy way.

How does it happen that any of these slaves manage to escape from the Treadmill and turn themselves into masters?

The answer is that very few really do escape. The overseer of the Treadmill, the dread spirit that some call *maya*, some the Devil or the Father of Lies, has many good tricks at his disposal. He has been around a long time and understands very well the inner weaknesses of the human race.

The Spirit of the Lie knows that his ancient adversary, the Spirit of Truth, can sometimes influence these hypnotized donkeys. It can give them a fleeting glimpse of reality and awaken them for a moment from the fog of dreams in which they habitually pass their time. There is, in the human psyche, a will to truth, but this will is weak compared with its opponent, the will to self-deception. The Spirit of Truth works through the will to truth.

But the Lying Spirit knows how to counteract and neutralize the will to truth before it enables the slaves to liberate themselves from their delusions. It does this by cunningly preparing a counterfeit, an imitation of the real Work, a fantasy Work. It is in this fantasy Work that so many of the slaves that try to escape become entrapped. The fantasy Work enables them to think that they are working on themselves when, in fact, they have merely swapped one set of dreams for another set.

In the diagram entitled *Stages of the Way*, the Treadmill is shown surrounded by the Forest. Slaves that escape from the Treadmill enter the Forest and must find their way through it before their real inner work can even begin. It is easy to get lost in the Forest, and many do. It is full of paths that lead nowhere and of guides that do not know the way themselves. It also contains the deep and gloomy gorge that Hermann Hesse called the *Morbio Inferiore* in which all inspiration is lost, enthusiasm vanishes, high aims are forgotten.(38)

Beyond the Forest, visible from time to time between the trees, are two lofty peaks, the Mountain of Power and the Mountain of Liberation. Glimpses of these peaks encourage the traveller to press on and try to find his way to the foot of the mountains. But the glimpses are only occasional and are all too easily forgotten. Having forgotten where he was trying to go, the traveller once again becomes lost.

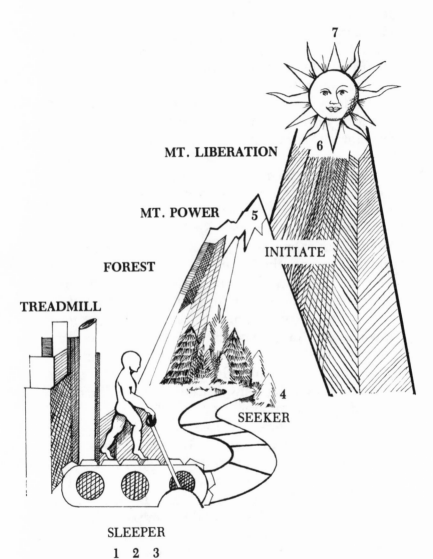

MT. LIBERATION

MT. POWER

FOREST

TREADMILL

INITIATE

SEEKER

SLEEPER
1 2 3

STAGES OF THE WAY

Because it is such a dangerous place the slaves that escape into the Forest are often worse off than before. At least in the Treadmill they were fairly comfortable and saved from knowing the truth about themselves by their prevailing state of hypnotized sleep. In the Forest, however, they are comfortable no longer. They cannot take refuge in their old delusions. They have seen glimpses of the truth and those glimpses have spoiled their sleep. They are neither happily enslaved nor really free. Their predicament was summed up by Gurdjieff in the following aphorism:

Happy is he who sits in his own chair; a thousand times happier is he who sits in the chair of the angels; but miserable is he who has no chair. (39)

Slaves who have escaped from the Treadmill and got lost in the Forest take refuge from their discomfort in the fantasy Work. They dream that they are "in the Work", but they are not. They have not paid their entrance fees. They have not sacrificed their dreams or conquered their mechanical habits. They are just as much slaves as they were before they left the Treadmill, but the grand illusion that they are "in the Work" prevents them from seeing this. They have entered the state called Second Sleep from which it is very difficult to awaken. People in Second Sleep dream that they are awake.

The pseudo-Work consists of a series of traps. Falling into any one of these traps will suffice to bring the real Work to a halt. Some people fall into one trap, some into another. Some manage, after long struggles, to escape from the traps. Others never escape for the simple reason that they do not know that they are trapped.

Who, then, can enter the real Work?

It is open only to full, dues-paying members of the SOT club. The letters SOT stand for Seekers of Truth. Members of the club are known collectively as the People of Truth. In Arabic, they are called the *Ahl-i-Haqq* and, as *Haqq* (truth) is one of the ninety-nine names of God, they can also be called the People of God. For members of the SOT club God is truth and the motto of the club places the search for truth above all other life aims.

I would rather know the truth, however terrible, than take refuge in some system of comforting delusions.

Although the SOT club is open to everyone very few people become members. This is because they cannot afford to pay the dues. To enter the SOT club and become a full member, one must sacrifice one's illusions, particularly one's illusions about oneself. This is what most people dare not do. Even those who have escaped from the Treadmill would often rather enter the fantasy Work and keep their illusions than enter the real Work and sacrifice them.

The fantasy Work takes the form of eight traps. Everyone who tries to enter the Work falls sooner or later into one of these traps. Such falls are inevitable. Any realistic follower of the Way knows this and prepares to confront the traps in advance. This involves knowing what they are, knowing if one has fallen into them, knowing how to get out.

Here are the characteristics of the eight major traps.

Trap #1. The Talk-Think Syndrome

This is a subtle trap and many fall into it. They talk about the Work. They think about the Work. But talking and thinking about Work will no more produce results than talking and thinking about sex will produce a baby. Actually the Work involves stopping the interior dialogue, but we, who have become accustomed to incessant inner chatter, do not feel comfortable in the silent state. We must talk to someone about something. If we cannot find anyone else to talk to we talk to ourselves.

This habit of talking about the Work is encouraged by the tendency of those who think they are "in the Work" to meet together in groups. Theoretically these groups are supposed to serve a useful purpose. They are intended to encourage the exchange of observations, to promote objectivity, sincerity, and so on. The groups rarely accomplish this because, in most cases, the last thing people in these groups want to do is to confront their own weaknesses. They are protected from such confrontations by an elaborate system of buffers and they have no intention of sacrificing those buffers.

To make matters worse, the people who lead such groups are, more often than not, completely ignorant of the science of types. Because of this ignorance they are in no position to understand the personal laws under which members of their group have to operate.

What with the ignorance of the average group leader and the reluctance of most of the group members to confront the monsters in their personal labyrinths, it is hardly surprising that such groups prove useless. They are in fact worse than useless because they encourage the talk-think syndrome. People imagine because they have spent some time talking about the Work, that they are therefore "in the Work". In actual fact, they often do not know what the Work is.

Trap #2. The Devotee Syndrome

An alternative name for this trap is the Starry-eyed Syndrome. It involves fanatical devotion to and blind belief in a teacher or a teaching. This devotion completely blinds the devotee. It destroys any capacity for objective mentation that its victim may at one time have possessed. All the emotions are focussed on the Master who attains the status of a god in the eyes of the devotee. The Master can do no wrong. The Master's teachings must be accepted quite literally and in their entirety. If the Master declares that there are two moons in the sky then there must be two moons despite the fact that no one has ever seen a trace of moon #2. If the Master says that there is a cosmic law which causes planets to grow into suns and suns to grow into galaxies this must surely happen despite the fact that it is a physical impossibility.

The Starry-eyed Syndrome is a powerful and dangerous trap. It is responsible for many of the self-imposed disasters that have afflicted the human race. The supremely dangerous human being is not the robber, the rapist or the ordinary murderer. It is the starry-eyed fanatic who, in the name of some system, political or religious, will gladly exterminate an entire population and be perfectly convinced that he is justified in so doing. Most of the atrocities of the 20th century have been committed by such people. Their capacity for destruction is unlimited. They are totally blinded by their belief systems. They have lost the capacity to think objectively and have destroyed in themselves the function of conscience.

All such fanatics are victims of two weaknesses, credulity and suggestibility, which Gurdjieff defined as the curse of the human race. If World War III ever starts it will not be the fault of bumbling militarists or of muddled politicians. It will be the work of fanatical devotees, perfectly willing to blow up the planet in the name of some half-baked doctrine in which they happen to believe.

Trap #3. The False Messiah Syndrome

This trap is the opposite of the Starry-eyed Syndrome. Those who fall into it become convinced that they are Masters, capable of transmitting to others certain vital truths about the spiritual life.

The category of False Messiah does not include what might be called conscious spiritual con-artists. Such people, quite deliberately, for their personal gain, start some phony religion and often do very well out of it. These are simply salesmen who traffic in dreams. Their activities can best be regarded as a branch of the entertainment industry.

The real victims of Trap #3 are quite sincere. They really believe in the claims they make. Generally they have had a religious experience of one sort or another. Perhaps they have been to India and picked up ideas from some guru. Perhaps they have taken drugs and had what is known as a psychedelic experience. Perhaps they have merely cobbled together ideas taken from here and there which they present as a system.

All the victims of Trap #3 have one thing in common. They are on an ego trip. They want followers, the more followers the better. This is the characteristic that distinguishes them from the real Masters. Genuine Masters never try to attract disciples. On the contrary, they tend to discourage them, warning them that the Way is difficult, that it is better to remain comfortably asleep than to become half awake.

A second feature of victims of the False Messiah Syndrome is that they will never let go of any of their followers. They want to keep them in a permanent state of dependence. So schools started by these phony Masters have one thing in common. No one in the school ever graduates. No one can leave of his or her own free will. The false Master makes slaves of his followers, exacts total obedience, discourages independent thought and action. Anyone who rebels against this slavery is regarded as a traitor.

The behavior of a genuine Master is the exact opposite. He encourages the student to rely on himself, to find his own way, to discover the teacher within himself. He will offer advice only if advice is asked for. He can hold up a mirror in which those who wish to see can see, but he will not attempt to force anyone to look in that mirror. He will make no attempt to hold on to any of his pupils. If they want to leave him, he will encourage them to go. He is not interested in surrounding himself with a group of hypnotized sheep who slavishly believe every word he says. He is concerned with liberation, not with substituting one form of slavery for another. He gets no satisfaction from dominating his followers. Such ego games do not interest him. Whether he has one pupil, a hundred pupils or no pupils is, for him, a matter of indifference.

Another characteristic of the phony Master is his conceit. This conceit takes various forms. The "Master" will dress himself in fancy robes and bestow on himself various lofty titles. He will call himself a god-man, a *maharishi*, a *bhagwan*, a high initiate, a magus. All his pupils must address him as Master and treat him with the utmost reverence.

The behavior of a genuine Master is the exact opposite. He spurns all titles and does not dress in fancy robes. Far from encouraging a reverent attitude on the part of his pupils, he will deliberately shock them by behaving in a manner seemingly unworthy of a Master. Being free of ego, he is genuinely indifferent as to whether other people admire him or not. He does not need their admiration. He has reached a point at which he can be neither flattered nor insulted.

Trap #4. The Organization Syndrome

This is a dangerous trap indeed and one into which whole groups of people are liable to fall. It plays an important part in the fantasy Work and might even be called the cornerstone of that Work.

The Organization Syndrome develops when a genuine Master dies and his older pupils consider it their duty, as they put it, to continue the Master's work. So they form an organization. They turn themselves into a hierarchy. Their rank in the hierarchy depends not on their personal level of being, but on the length of time they have been in the Work and their closeness to the Master when he was still alive.

Such hierarchies tend to become fossilized. They discourage independence and freedom of thought and take refuge in a rigid orthodoxy. Everything the Master taught becomes sacred even if it was obviously rubbish put forward to test the level of a pupil's credulity. All the methods that the Master used must be transmitted exactly as he taught them.

These "pillars of orthodoxy" never take notice of the fact that times change, that people change, that methods that proved effective in one place and time may not prove effective in another place and time. They also fail to realize that, in the Work, seniority is not equivalent to spiritual progress. The fact that one has been forty or fifty years "in the Work" or that one once knew the Master intimately does not make one a liberated being.

The so-called older people in the Work may long ago have lost any real understanding of the aims of the Work. They may be operating on autopilot, quite mechanically. They know all the standard phrases and the approved techniques and can trot these out effortlessly whenever someone pushes the right button. They appear, for this reason, to have authority, and younger people who enter the organization can easily be brainwashed into thinking that they do have authority.

The fact is, however, that the older people are spiritually often at a dead end. They have become stuck in the Morbio Inferiore. Having lost sight of the real aims of the Work, they occupy themselves with organization politics. They expend their energies on the little games of one upmanship that go on in any organization. They are not Masters but small time politicians.

Actually it is doubtful if anyone can, as is said, continue the Master's work. A genuine Master will develop his own methods which will accord with his special interests and abilities. Gurdjieff, for example, was, as he himself put it, a teacher of dancing. He taught through movements. Certainly this was not the only way in which he taught but the movements played an important part in his methods.

Another Master might place emphasis on some different form of work, on meditation, on outer or inner theater, on breathing exercises and so on. There are many techniques, some suitable for people of one type, some for another. But the "pillars of orthodoxy," who consider it their duty to "continue the Master's work" fail to realize that the approach taught by the Master may not be suitable for present day conditions. Nor do they pause to ask themselves whether they themselves have understood the Master's teaching.

The Organization Syndrome is just as bad for the pupils that develop it as it is for the members of the hierarchy who run the organization. It is bad for the pupils because it offers them a means of deceiving themselves, a hiding place, a subterfuge, a piece of trickery. Because they are members of the club, they think they have accomplished something. They are, as they think, "in the Work". They go to group meetings, they do movements, they belong. If they stick around long enough, they will rise in the hierarchy and become group leaders. They may end up imagining that they are Masters themselves.

Unfortunately all these activities of the organization can become completely mechanical. They have little or no effect on those that do them just as their once weekly church attendance often has little or no effect on those who go to church. For such people church going has become a habit. On Sunday one goes to church just as on Saturday night one may eat out at a restaurant or go to a movie.

It is exceedingly difficult to escape from the Organization Trap both for members of the hierarchy who run the organization and for the neophytes they are supposed to be guiding. Many people like this trap and are happy to stay in it. They prefer the fantasy Work to the real Work. They like to be told what to think and what to do. It saves them from the trouble of trying to think for themselves.

It does sometimes happen that, within such a moribund organization, a genuine Master develops, with power enough to break open the trap and release those caught in it, assuming that they want to be released. This happened in the Theosophical Society when Krishnamurti, who was a genuine Master, shattered the organization that had been prepared for him (the Order of the Star) and ruthlessly exposed the pretenses underlying that particular example of the fantasy Work. It required great courage on the part of Krishnamurti to do that but his possession of that sort of courage is one characteristic of the genuine Master. He is a breaker of idols, a shatterer of dreams, a destroyer of ready-made belief systems, an enemy of orthodoxies and a distruster of hierarchies. He himself is a free spirit and his only interest is to help others to attain freedom.

Trap #5. The Personal Salvation Syndrome

This is a subtle and dangerous trap. It has been the curse of all three Abrahamic religions, Judaism, Christianity and Islam. It has tended to turn all these religions into guilt cults in which grovelling devotees implore their god to forgive them for their sins and to grant them something vaguely described as salvation. Salvation from what? From hell presumably. From the fire everlasting, which is one of those pernicious devices that the priests of these religions have invented to frighten their followers into behaving as the priests think they ought to behave.

One great error underlies the Personal Salvation Syndrome. Those who suffer from it imagine that the personal self, the so-called ego, can be either saved or damned. If they go to heaven, it will be the personal self, Mr. or Mrs. Jones, that will be hoisted aloft among the harps and angels. If they fall into hell, it will again be Mr. or Mrs. Jones who shrieks and groans amid the devils and the everlasting fire. So the lives of the aforesaid Mr. and Mrs. Jones, dominated as they are by this absurd superstition, become pervaded by a sense of guilt and sin and a misplaced craving for personal salvation.

Real salvation involves becoming liberated from the personal self and the narrow confines of the ego. The kingdom of heaven, in so far as this much abused phrase means anything, refers to this state of liberation from ego. We can no more enter the kingdom of heaven wearing our egos than the gospel camel can pass through the needle's eye. Worrying about "what shall I do to be saved" merely makes a bad situation worse. "I" cannot be saved. "I" is the obstacle, the creator of the great illusion of separateness.

The real Work involves a struggle to separate from this I, to transcend the narrow ego, to attain union with the higher Self, which is real and impersonal and outside time-space. "He who sees the Self in all things and all things in the Self, he is liberated." Being liberated, he is no longer concerned with his personal fate. He does not bother to ask whether he is saved or damned, whether he will go, after death, to heaven or hell. For him, all ideas about heaven or hell are fairy tales only fit for children. Once the personal self has been shed, all talk about what shall I do to be saved becomes meaningless. There can be no salvation for the personal self because it is based on an illusion.

Trap #6. The Super-effort Syndrome.

This subtle trap can also be called the Climb-Mount-Everest Syndrome. It consists in the belief that the Work involves some frightfully intense super-effort analogous to the effort made by a mountaineer who struggles to climb Mount Everest single handed.

The trap is subtle because the idea behind it is close to the truth. The Work does involve great effort, but it is a very special kind of effort. This effort involves the maintenance of balance and awareness. It is more like the skill of a ropewalker or a juggler than the sort of heroic teeth-clenching efforts involved in feats of derring-do such as climbing Mount Everest.

Underlying the Super-effort Syndrome is a deeply rooted misunderstanding about the nature of the Work. The real Work consists of a struggle against the state of identification. Identification means becoming totally immersed in what one is doing and in losing all objective awareness of one's own existence. Many people pass their entire lives in this state, and our culture is designed to ensure its continuance. We are encouraged at all times to become identified with something, with a dream, a project, a belief, a game, an ambition, a craving. We are so accustomed to being identified that we can hardly believe that it is possible to live in any other way.

It is quite possible for people to become identified with what they imagine to be the Work. This causes them to approach the Work in a grim and earnest spirit. They think they must demand of themselves not ordinary efforts but super-efforts. They do not understand that the Work is a game of skill to be played lightly in a spirit of detachment. For them, the Work turns into a sort of ordeal.

This grim attitude produces feelings of tension and discomfort. Any failure to persist in super-efforts produces a sense of guilt. The guilt feelings generate those patterns of self-punishment that have been and still are so unpleasant a feature of the lives of certain kinds of religious fanatics.

These fanatics punish themselves by such procedures as wearing hair shirts, fasting, practicing sexual abstinence, wearing chains, not sleeping, self-flagellation and so on. They often develop a pernicious habit of punishing others who happen not to agree with their religious beliefs. It was such punitive excesses that moved the Roman poet to exclaim, *"Tantum religio potuit suadere malorum"*, (so great is the evil that religion is able to arouse).

The Super-effort Syndrome produces another more subtle effect. Organizers of the Work, who often get caught in this trap, will set aside a period of time to be devoted to super-effort. Everything is planned to make life during this time as difficult and unpleasant as possible. There are interminable readings from various sacred books, intensive spells of hard manual labor, special exercises supposed to promote self-remembering. There may be very little food, not much sleep, no heating in winter, harsh conditions generally. An attitude of grim determination prevails. Do or die. Conquer or perish.

It is possible for those who understand what they are doing to gain something from these endurance tests. The trouble is that many involved in the test do not understand what they are doing. The test then becomes an excuse for an ego trip. A competitive spirit develops to see who can suffer most discomfort without complaining.

The real damage starts after the orgy of self-imposed suffering ends. There is a reaction. The energy gained, instead of being used creatively, is dissipated in those very indulgences that were renounced during the period of deprivation. The people involved feel entitled to indulge. Have they not been making super-efforts? Are they not, therefore, entitled to relax and enjoy themselves? So they squander all that they have gained in useless, and often, harmful activities.

The Super-effort Syndrome prevents those that suffer from it from understanding the nature of the real Work. The Work is not heroic and does not involve spectacular feats of daring. It is comparable to the patient, skillful exertions of one who carves and shapes some difficult material, the worker in stone or ivory. It involves repeated small efforts rather than one great effort. It involves endless patience, a willingness to start over and over again. Above all it involves freedom from identification, for identification always destroys the real Work and

replaces it with the fantasy Work. It does this in so
subtle a way that many who fall into this trap are
quite unable to see where they have made their
mistake.

Trap #7. The Sunday-Go-To-Meeting Syndrome

This is one of the more obvious traps. It is closely
linked to the Organization Trap and cannot operate
without an organization. Those who fall into the
trap lose sight of their real aim. For real work on
themselves, they substitute regular attendance at
meetings of the organization. They attend these
meetings quite mechanically, out of habit. By
attending them, they get a feeling of belonging and
an assurance that they are really "in the Work".
When they are at a meeting, they make the
appropriate noises, trot out an observation or two,
listen to lectures, readings and so on. Once they
leave the meeting, they forget about the Work.

In such people, the Work has become a
manifestation of personality. It is entirely artificial.
At one time, presumably, it did mean something
real but they have long ago lost all contact with that
reality. Their work is based on fantasy, pure and
simple. It is a product of the mechanism for creating
illusions which operates so relentlessly and so subtly
in the human brain.

Trap #8. The Hunt-the-Guru Syndrome.

This, too, is a rather obvious trap. Those that fall into it spend their lives going from teacher to teacher, demanding from each that he reveal to them the secrets of the Work. They cannot or will not understand that there are no secrets that can be revealed. The secrets of the Work protect themselves. They can be discovered only through practice, and that practice must reach a certain level of intensity and continuity before the secret can be discovered.

Those who fall into the Hunt-the-Guru Trap have no intention of practicing either intensely or continuously. They want everything presented to them on a platter. If the Work is not presented in this way they conclude that the guru was a fraud and wander off in search of someone else. Their search never ends, or rather it ends only with their deaths, for the simple reason that they do not want it to end. For them the hunt has become a game in itself. They have long ago forgotten what they were hunting for.

III

THE REAL WORK

Knowledge, Power and Wisdom

Real Work involves the development of knowledge and power.

Knowledge without power gives no results. Power without knowledge gives wrong results. Wisdom emerges from the balanced interaction of knowledge and power.

Knowledge and wisdom are different things. Our technological culture is overloaded with knowledge. We know a lot about almost everything except ourselves. We cannot convert this mass of information into wisdom because we have not understood the need to raise our level of consciousness.

The Work involves acquisition of a special kind of knowledge. If it is to be converted into wisdom this knowledge must be digested. It cannot be digested by the ordinary patterns of thinking. To digest it we must learn to think holistically.

Holistic thinking is difficult. It involves thinking about whole systems and seeing the connections between holons at different levels. There are many of these levels. Subatom, atom, molecule, organelle, organism, ecosystem, biosphere, planet, sun, galaxy, all these are holons. All interact. All must be taken into account.

Holistic thinking is, for the most part, non-verbal. It uses symbols, moving hieroglyphs. The words it does use are kept to a minimum. Key ideas that cannot be expressed as diagrams are formulated in aphorisms, brief sayings that condense the maximum amount of information in the minimum amount of words. These are the aphorisms of the neo-gnostics.

1. Define your life aims.
2. Conserve and concentrate *chi*. Your life depends on it.
3. Learn how to convert your knowledge into wisdom.

4. Stop dreaming; be here now.
5. Breathe consciously.
6. Control the Horse, care for the Carriage, awaken the Driver, discover the Master.
7. Substitute intentional doing for accidental happening.
8. Do only what is necessary.
9. Maintain a watchman at the gate of impressions.
10. In activities learn to see the play of three forces.
11. Believe nothing; test everything.
12. Distinguish between the higher will and the lower wills.
13. Strength exerted gives more strength; weakness indulged gives greater weakness.
14. Separate from all the manifestations of your machine.
15. Distinguish the quality of essence from that of the *persona*.
16. Stand on the bank of time's river and watch the flow.

To these aphorisms must be added a number of diagrams or *arcana*. Some of these are as follows:

1. The Universal Mandala.
2. The Stages of the Way.
3. The Pyramid of Being and Knowledge.
4. Horse, Carriage, Driver and Master.
5. The Diagram of Fate.

Defining Aim

Those who wish to be realistic about the Work must begin by defining their aim. This need is expressed in the following aphorism:

Unless you know where you want to go, you cannot take the first step on the journey.

How shall we define our aim?

I am a slave; I aim to become a master.
I live in a world of dreams; I aim to enter the real world.
I am enmeshed in lies; I aim to know the truth.
I am many; I aim to become one.
I am a separate ego; I aim to blend with the All.

Such definitions refer to long term aims. They are too general and too vague to provide a basis for practical day to day work.

This Work is both an art and a science. It is creative and, in this sense, is analogous to the work of a craftsman, an artist or a builder. But it is also exploratory, analogous to the work of a research scientist.

The central truth is that we do not know ourselves and for this reason, are not masters of ourselves. So the Work has to begin with a long period of self-observation. But who will do the observing? We are a multiplicity, a swarm of I's, many of which have conflicting aims. We need an Observer who will observe objectively and learn who is who in the zoo. But how does one go about creating the Observer?

Observer and Deputy Steward

At this point we seem to confront a paradox. The Observer does not exist. We have to create it. But who is "we"? The allegory of the house full of disorderly servants suggests that the servants can select one of their number to act as a Deputy Steward and maintain some sort of order until the Master appears.(40) But who chooses the Deputy Steward and from what source does this entity draw its power?

We can only conclude that the Deputy Steward elects itself. He or she is the only one among the servants who has an understanding of priorities. The other servants have their own preferred life aims and life games. One wants to play the Money Game, another the Fame Game, another may fancy the Science Game or the Art Game. But the Deputy Steward understands that the only game really worth playing is the Master Game, (41) and that all the other games have to take second place. He is in the difficult position of having to explain this fact to the other servants who are often rebellious and unwilling to accept his authority.

Conserving Chi

Now we ask, from what source can the Deputy Steward draw power? Or, to put the question somewhat differently, how can the Observer develop that capacity for objective observation which it needs if it is to function efficiently? The answer to this question is given by the aphorism:

Conserve and concentrate chi. Your life depends on it.

Chi is a special energy-substance which gives us the power *intentionally* to focus our awareness. It is called *chi* in Chinese and *ki* in Japanese. There seems to be no word for it in English. *Chi* is generated in the body during the hours of sleep. We awaken with a certain supply. Once that supply is dissipated, it is hard to replenish. (42)

Chi endows the Observer with the capacity to observe objectively what goes on. It makes possible the state of double awareness that is the basis of self-remembering. Through the application of chi, we can separate from the various manifestations of our machines. We can observe, without becoming identified, our thoughts, movements and emotions. In alchemical terms *chi* is the great transforming agent through which base metals can be turned into gold.

As long as we conserve *chi* we can observe ourselves and separate from the manifestations of our machines. Once we allow our supply of *chi* to dissipate, we are helpless. We become the playthings of our impressions, our emotions, our dreams.

Chi gives us the power to catch our impressions before they engage our inner machinery. As long as our *chi* is not dissipated we can protect ourselves from the impact of casual impressions. This function of *chi* is expressed by the aphorism:

*Maintain a watchman at the
gate of impressions.*

It is difficult for us to avoid dissipating our daily supply of *chi*. As soon as we wake in the morning, we are assailed by day dreams which replace the night dreams from which we have just emerged. We rarely awaken with a clear awareness of our own presence. We plunge, instead, into a stream of associative thinking that is likely to continue through the day. As soon as this daydreaming begins our *chi* drains out of us. We may lose our entire supply during the first hour of the day. For this reason it is necessary, as soon as we awaken, to begin a special exercise calculated to prevent this loss of awareness.

Breathing and Repetition

This exercise is designed to prevent the wastage of *chi*. It has been stated by many teachers that *chi* is derived from the air we breathe, by an intentional process that extracts it from that air. (43) This intentional process involves centering the awareness on the heart and following the breath as it flows into the lungs. By lowering the focus of our awareness, we create a new center of being. We emerge from the *persona* and enter the essence.

This process of centering in the essence by lowering the focus of awareness is called "entering the cave of the heart". The cave of the heart is not in the physical heart but is a new center of being felt to be near the heart.

Awareness of breathing can only be effective if the face is kept relaxed. The facial muscles are the seat of the *persona*, named for the mask that Greek actors wore to portray tragedy or comedy. As long as our center of awareness is located in the face, we are living, so to speak, on the surface of our selves. Living thus on the surface, we are at the mercy of every wind that blows. An unpleasant impression, a word spoken in anger or scorn, a disturbing memory is enough to destroy our calm. By learning to center our awareness at a deeper level, we attain greater stability.

Repetition can be linked to the rhythm of breathing. Used in this way, it will prevent the flood of associative thinking from occupying the center of our awareness. The technique of repetition is very old. It is the basis of *mantra* yoga and of various religious practices.

A *mantra* is a focusing device. It has no virtue in itself. It helps to exclude wandering thoughts. It can also have a certain deeper significance. For example, the two mantric syllables AUM and HUM correspond to the cosmic flow in the course of which worlds become manifest and unmanifest. AUM, the outbreathing, corresponds to the process of manifestation. HUM, the inbreathing, corresponds to the opposite process.

The AUM-HUM *mantra*, because of its simplicity, is one of the easiest to use. HUM should accompany the inbreath, AUM the outbreath.

The three syllables, BE HERE NOW, (44) also constitute a *mantra*. This *mantra* was chosen by Ram Dass (Richard Alpert) as a title for his book on the Work. He chose well. If rightly used, this mantra has great power. Each syllable has significance, and that significance must be remembered by those who would use the *mantra* effectively.

BE stands for the awareness of presence, awareness not only of the breath but of the whole body, its posture, state of relaxation or tension, and so on.

HERE stands for awareness of place, where one is.

NOW stands for awareness of time, of this particular moment in the stream of events.

Presence, time, place, these are the three components of being. Awareness of these three is the essential feature of the state called self-remembering.

Loss of Aim

Remember yourself always, everywhere.

This aphorism is more easily said than done. Self-remembering should be the basis of our practice but in actual life that practice becomes very sporadic. Again and again, awareness of breathing is lost. The *mantra* is displaced by a flood of associative thinking. The face becomes tense. The center of being leaves the cave of the heart and locates in the mask of the *persona*. The little ego takes the place of the real Self and starts to fuss and fret, squandering precious *chi* in the process.

What can we do about it?

First it is necessary to realize that this will happen. Again and again, in the course of the day, we will become identified. The watchman at the gate will fall asleep. All sorts of casual impressions, day dreams, random thoughts will occupy our awareness. Instead of being centered, we will become scattered, blown about like a leaf in the wind. Our *chi* will be dissipated. We will end the day exhausted, feeling that we have accomplished absolutely nothing. We may even entertain serious doubts as to whether anything can be accomplished by the way of the inner Work. Perhaps the whole idea of the Work is one more example of our almost infinite capacity for deluding ourselves.

Such thoughts lead us directly into that "gloomy gorge" which Hesse called the Morbio Inferiore. Aim is lost. Inspiration dies. A feeling of futility replaces our sense of direction. The great project, the "Journey to the East," loses its meaning.

At this point it becomes necessary for the Deputy Steward, or the Observer, to call for a meeting of all the other servants. The central question of life aim has to be reconsidered. What do the other servants really want? To go back to the Treadmill? To turn themselves once again into blindfolded donkeys? To lose sight altogether of the great peaks, the Mountains of Power and Liberation, and spend the rest of their lives going round in circles, lost in dreams, dominated by illusions? How could such a retrograde step be justified? Having set out on the journey, how can one afford to go back? It would surely be better to perish on the Way than to allow oneself to drift back into the Treadmill.

But the other servants are rebellious. They have their own aims. This one wants to make money. That one wants to do scientific research. Another wants fame. Another wants to create great works of art.

Very well, says the Observer, and now hear this.

There is no legitimate life aim that cannot be attained more surely if one is awake. To be awake is everything.

It is the function of the Observer, who is the forerunner of the Master, to convince the other servants of the truth of this aphorism. We gain nothing, absolutely nothing, by passing our lives in a state of hypnotized sleep. Sleep of this kind is not only unpleasant. It is dangerous. In sleep one does not know who one is, where one is or what one is doing. One is blind. One trips over obstacles. One makes mistakes.

To be awake is everything.

It is the proper function of the Observer to reason in this way with the other servants. He does not need to tyrannize, to threaten them with hell fire or damnation. He simply says "choose". Choose between slavery and freedom, between seeing and being blind, between having control and being pushed around by outside forces. The Observer operates by reason, not by threats.

But one thing must be remembered. We have only a limited amount of time in which to create this very special entity we call the Observer. We can be said to have entered the Work only when we have created it and endowed it with enough power to enable it to control the other servants.

Power is developed through practice, through steady, unrelenting effort, day after day, week after week. In this respect, the Work is like any other special skill, such as the skill required to play a difficult musical instrument. "If I fail to practice for a day," said a famous concert pianist, "I notice the difference. If I fail to practice for two days, my wife notices the difference. If I fail to practice for a week, even the audience notices the difference."

The inner Work involves greater effort than does learning to master the piano because the human body is a much more complex instrument. This fact is often overlooked. People imagine they can become Masters by attending a meeting once a week, by doing a few movements, by indulging once a year in some sort of heroics which they describe as making super-efforts. All this is part of the fantasy Work and can only result in self-deception. The real Work involves constantly repeated effort, a never ending struggle with identification. We become identified again and again in the course of the day and must drag ourselves back and remember. Only in this way can any permanent change be brought about. Hence the aphorism:

Until your practice reaches a certain level of intensity and continuity you will not attain any permanent results.

The Higher Will

The Observer soon discovers that he has no real will. The house is at the mercy of a swarm of unruly servants, each of which wants to run the show.

There are as many wills as there are servants. What passes for will is merely the resultant of desires.

The possibility exists, however, of developing real will. This higher will can gradually dominate the lower wills. The lower wills push people now in one direction, now in another. They correspond to a conflicting variety of desires, desire for money, for fame, for sex, for possessions and so on. Any one of these desires can temporarily become dominant and take charge of the machinery.

The higher will pushes people in one direction only, from sleep to awakening, from weakness to strength. It has three components, the will to power (over oneself, not over others), the will to truth and the will to self-transcendence. (45) These three components must be kept in balance. The will to power can easily become ego centered and turn into a desire to dominate others. The will to truth can be replaced by credulity, by the "will to believe". The will to upward self-transcendence can be replaced by the will to downward self-transcendence.

The will to downward self-transcendence is particularly dangerous. Those who develop this will become fanatical members of some organization and blindly follow whatever line of conduct it demands. It is this will to downward self-transcendence that gives power to the various groups of terrorists that play so conspicuous a role in the modern world. They will do anything, including blowing up the planet, in the name of the cause with which they have become identified. The will to downward self-transcendence is a terrifying phenomenon.

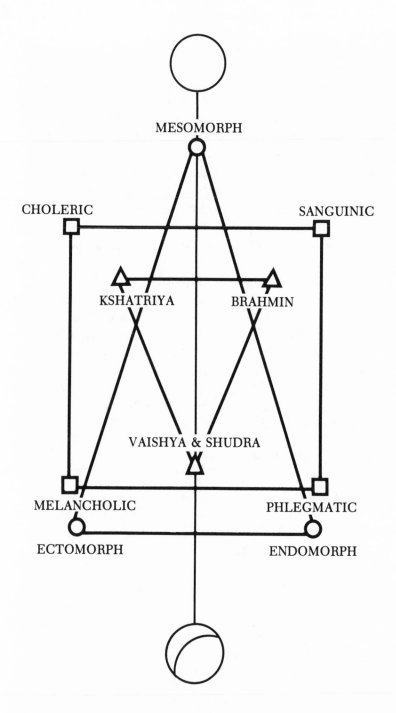

DIAGRAM OF TYPES

Development of the higher will marks the beginning of the real inner Work. Until we develop that will our work is unstable. We have built our inner temple on sand. Any flood can sweep away the whole structure. Only after the higher will has been developed can we start to build a durable structure. We have dug our way down to bedrock. The Observer, who is both the architect and the builder of the inner temple, now has real power. It is able to do more than merely observe. It is beginning to turn into the Master.

Sunpath, Moonpath

Higher will is developed by the struggle between yes and no, between the Force Affirming and the Force Denying. The struggle can take place within any of our functions. It may be physical, emotional or intellectual. It may involve all these functions simultaneously. It may take the form of a struggle with some mechanical habit, with physical laziness, emotional instability, intellectual fuzziness or various manifestations of the *persona*, referred to collectively as character defects.

The struggle between yes and no is expressed symbolically by the dyad which forms the central pillar of the Diagram of Types, also called the Diagram of Fate. This dyad has many manifestations, male-female, yin-yang, active-passive and so on. But the aspect which applies to the process of developing will is called the Sunpath-Moonpath. This dyad determines the fate of every man or woman.

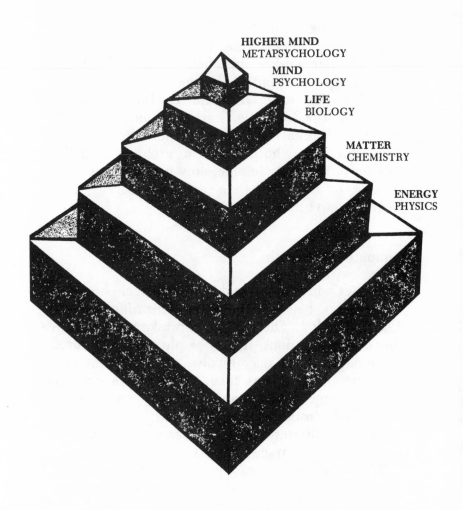

HIGHER MIND
METAPSYCHOLOGY

MIND
PSYCHOLOGY

LIFE
BIOLOGY

MATTER
CHEMISTRY

ENERGY
PHYSICS

PYRAMID OF KNOWLEDGE AND BEING

The Sunpath represents the way of light and the way of effort. Those who follow the Sunpath swim *against* the current which flows downhill in the direction of ever greater disorder (entropy). It is a law that, in our universe, entropy must increase with the flow of time. On a small scale, however, this decline can be reversed. The working of a cosmic law gives to certain beings the chance, if they choose to do so, to swim against this current. By swimming against the current they ascend on the Pyramid of Being and enter the higher hierarchy.

The Pyramid of Being and Knowledge

This is one of the key diagrams. It shows the five major holons that constitute all and everything in our megalocosmos. These five major holons—energy, matter, life, mind, higher mind—correspond to the five major branches of knowledge. These are physics, chemistry, biology, psychology and metapsychology.

We are concerned with metapsychology, the science of the self-transformation of Man. In our culture this is a neglected science. It is not taught in our universities. Nonetheless, it is vitally important. Unless we develop a better understanding of this science we may perish.

The basic theory of metapsychology is that Man is an unfinished being endowed with the capacity to complete his own evolution. Every man or woman has the opportunity to test whether this theory is true or false. Very few do test it because the only way in which one can do so is to use oneself as one's

| HORSE | CARRIAGE | DRIVER | MASTER |
| EMOTIONS | BODY | INTELLECT | HIGHER SELF |

THE CONVEYANCE

own experimental animal. The great experiment confronts one at the outset with a choice. Shall I follow the Moonpath and go downhill with the flow, or shall I follow the Sunpath and rise to a higher level on the cosmic hierarchy? A person's fate depends on which of these paths he or she follows.

Horse, Carriage, Driver, Master (46)

The struggle between yes and no involves all the parts of our being. We can use the allegory of the conveyance, Horse, Carriage, Driver and Master, to designate these parts. The Driver stands for the intellect, the Horse for the emotions, the Carriage for the physical body. The Master who should ride in the Carriage and tell the Driver where to go is not there. His place can be taken by the Observer. The Observer, if it develops enough power, will turn into the Master.

If real will is to be developed each of the three components of the conveyance, Horse, Carriage and Driver, must be disciplined and strengthened. During this process, there takes place in each part a struggle between yes and no. Always we are tempted to follow the way of weakness and overlook our bad habits, but unless we resist this temptation we will never develop real will. The struggle between yes and no takes different forms in each of the three components.

Care of the Carriage

A common delusion of people who have allowed
the fantasy Work to replace the real Work relates to
the care of the Carriage (the physical body). Such
people imagine that they can indulge in all sorts of
harmful physical habits, that they can use drugs,
including alcohol and tobacco, take little or no
physical exercise, eat all the wrong foods and
generally neglect their health and still build within
their bodies the inner Temple.

If such people are challenged, they invariably
come up with excuses. They say they are not
interested in the body which is merely a vehicle for
their lofty souls. As for their bad physical habits,
they could get rid of them if they wanted to, but
they don't want to. This cop-out is especially
favored by those addicted to tobacco. Students of
drug addiction are well aware that tobacco
smoking, particularly cigarette smoking, produces a
very subtle form of slavery. It is not a crude form of
physical dependence like heroin addiction. Those
who decide to free themselves from this slavery do
not suffer from obvious withdrawal symptoms.
They do not sweat, vomit, suffer from sleeplessness,
have convulsions. They simply feel a craving for
nicotine and the craving is so strong that many who
try to free themselves give up the attempt.

The cigarette habit seems common among people
who imagine that they are "in the Work" and their
attitude to their addiction provides a clear example
of the hypocrisy that characterizes all those who
have substituted fantasy for reality. If you challenge
them they laugh and pretend that it does not really

matter. Of course they could kick the habit if they chose to but they don't choose to. Or they refer to some pillar in the Work, "so-and-so smoked like a chimney. If it was all right for him, it is for me." So they lie to themselves. The fact is, of course, that they have no real will, and are following the Moonpath while convincing themselves that they are following the Sunpath.

All sorts of people who live unhealthy life styles claim to be working on themselves when they obviously are not. The real Work calls for the maintenance, not of ordinary health, but of super-health. This involves more than the avoidance of harmful practices. Aerobic exercises designed to increase the capacity of the lungs and to strengthen the heart should be combined with stretching exercises to promote flexibility. Only a properly trained, flexible body will last for the full human life span of a hundred years. It is natural for those in the Work to try to attain this full span. They need all the time they can get to complete the building of the inner Temple.

Proper food intake is another aspect of the care of the carriage that is all too often neglected. We are primates, closely related to the apes. Apes are predominantly vegetarians. The gorilla sustains its huge body on a diet of bamboo shoots. The human primate can also live on a purely vegetarian diet. Fruit, nuts, cereal grains and legumes can provide all the raw materials the body needs both to repair itself and to fuel its various functions.

But we are also hunting primates. We learned very early in our history to kill our fellow creatures and eat their bodies. This habit of killing became a part of our nature and is responsible for many of our more unpleasant characteristics. The modern American is predominantly a corpse eater. He consumes large amounts of red meat with results which are often disastrous. Huge quantities of corn and soy beans, which would make excellent human food, are wastefully converted into animal flesh to satisfy the meat guzzlers. These, by their meat-eating excesses, clog their arteries with cholesterol and add to their chances of developing cancer of the lower bowel.

Any one who is serious about the Work will avoid this practice, first because it is wasteful, second because it is harmful to the body, third because meat cannot be made available without violence and bloodshed. Those who doubt this should try killing a cow, a sheep or a pig. Most people are far too squeamish to slaughter animals themselves, but have no hesitation in letting others do the dirty work for them.

A perfectly adequate diet for the human animal can be created using fruit, nuts, vegetables, cereal grains and legumes. The addition of powdered milk will enhance its content of mineral elements and vitamins. Those who must have animal food can add small amounts of fish.

Another aspect of the care of the carriage relates to the sleep-waking cycle. There are two systems in the brain, the *ergotropic* and the *trophotropic* . The *ergotropic* system arouses the brain to activity, the *trophotropic* urges it to rest. Both are necessary and they must be balanced. Excessive activity produces a tense, nervous individual who lives always on the edge of exhaustion. Too much rest produces a dull heavy creature who seems only half alive.

During sleep the *trophotropic* system is dominant. Sleep has two levels, dreamless sleep and dreaming sleep. In dreamless sleep there is total relaxation. Many vitally important repairs of the body are brought about during this state. Dreaming sleep is a curious state characterized by rapid movements of the eyes and typical brain wave patterns. It seems to be necessary for the health of the organism though we do not know exactly why.

People vary greatly in their need for sleep. The nervous, habitually tense ectomorph sleeps badly and must spend more time in bed than the relaxed endomorph who sleeps deeply and easily. Those who understand their own type will know how much sleep they really need.

Controlling the Horse

The Horse, the animal in the brain that generates our emotions, is a difficult beast to understand and a hard one to control. It is nervous, unruly, irrational, prone to attacks of panic, to sudden impulses, to displays of anger, fear, jealousy and hate. Its behavior is further complicated by the fact that, in the human animal, the sex function is strongly linked to the emotions. Instead of being a purely instinctive function triggered mainly by the sense of smell and regulated by the changing seasons, the sex function in Man invades the other centers, exerting a disturbing influence both on the thoughts and on the emotions. It certainly contributes to the wild behavior of the Horse which is quite unruly enough without that.

For the purposes of the Work, the cooperation of the Horse is essential. A purely intellectual approach to the Work will give no results. It is the Horse (the emotions) that pulls the carriage. The emotions are the seat of the will, and without will we can do nothing. But the Observer who has to take charge of the conveyance in the absence of the Master cannot talk to the Horse because the Horse has no spoken language. It will respond to gestures, is sensitive to tone of voice. It reacts very rapidly. A word spoken in anger, a threatening gesture, are all that is needed to set the Horse rearing and kicking.

To make matters worse, the Horse communicates its panics to the Driver. This is due to the fact that thoughts and emotions are closely linked. So a thought can produce an emotion and an emotion can generate a thought. This is particularly true of negative emotions. They generate floods of negative thoughts. These in turn generate more negative emotions. A vicious circle results which can have disastrous effects.

The Observer who must struggle to remain aloof from these perturbations may find it almost impossible to calm the Horse. He can, however, struggle with the negative imaginings of the Driver. To do this he can make use of repetition, replacing the stream of negative inner talk with a *mantra*. Once the inner talk stops, he can try to quiet the Horse.

How does one teach good behavior to a panicky flighty beast that is always either running away from something it fears or chasing after something it desires? The Judeo-Christian guilt cult had a short way with the Horse. The Horse was the enemy. It was the Devil's agent. It embodied the lusts of the flesh and the pride of life. The only way to teach the animal to behave was to punish it. Abstain, abstain, abstain. Deny the Horse its pleasures. Try to pretend that it does not even exist.

Needless to say, this approach produced a rich crop of neuroses. You do not persuade the Horse to behave nicely either by beating it or by ignoring its needs. The right approach is the one taken by any skillful trainer of animals. Such a trainer learns to communicate with his subjects by tone of voice and gesture. He uses positive rather than negative reinforcement to encourage them to perform in the way he wishes.

This approach can be taken by the Observer once he has learned not to identify with the manifestations of the Horse. In the state of non-identification, he can step back and study the animal's emotional reactions objectively. The Observer has to learn to separate from his own emotional states. The capacity to say "*it* feels emotions" rather than "*I* feel an emotion" marks the achievement of a definite stage in the Work.

Laws Escapable and Inescapable

Strive to live under as few laws as possible.

This aphorism leads us to ask what is meant by laws. There are man-made laws and natural laws. Man-made laws vary from age to age and from culture to culture. Natural laws are universal and do not change.

Some natural laws are imposed by cosmic rhythms such as the alternation of day and night and the succession of the seasons. Others are imposed by the demands of the body, the need for activity and the need for rest, the need for fuel and for the building blocks out of which the body is constructed. These needs constitute laws from which we cannot escape. They apply to everyone everywhere.

More subtle and variable are the laws imposed by the essence. We are all programmed and our program is in the essence, not in the *persona*. Our essence program is one of the factors that shapes our fate. Other fate determinants are the place and time of our birth, the nature of our parents, the large scale historical processes happening at the time of our appearance. These all impose laws on us, many of which are inescapable. The laws imposed by our essence are also inescapable. We can no more change our essence laws than we can change the color of our eyes or our physical type.

Does this mean that our fate is predetermined, that we are compelled by our inborn mechanisms to behave in certain ways? To some extent it does. We cannot escape from the limitations imposed by our essence. A person with no ear for music will never become a great concert pianist. Someone with no aptitude for mathematics will never become a great theoretical physicist. When we say someone is "gifted" or "talented" we refer to essence characteristics, to powers that have been given. If those powers have not been given, they may be almost impossible to acquire.

What bearing does this have on the inner Work? Is aptitude for this Work another essence characteristic? It is difficult to answer this question. All we can say is that those that are drawn to the real Work have some essence need that must be satisfied. For such people, the Work appears to be the only life game worth playing. They will go on seeking the real Work until they find it.

It is perfectly possible for people to be attracted to the Work through the *persona*. They dream of developing higher powers, of becoming great teachers and so on. Such people will have no use for the real Work and will substitute for it the Work in fantasy.

Learn to separate persona from essence.

If we wish to understand which laws are, for us, escapable and which are inescapable, we must make this separation. Personality is artificial, essence is real. Laws imposed by the personality are escapable, those imposed by the essence are not.

Some of the components of essence are shown in the *Diagram of Types*. Some, but not all. Type is a complex phenomenon and some of its components are hard to measure. Following W.H. Sheldon, (47) we can present the triad of somatotypes with three components, *endomorphy*, *mesomorphy* and *ectomorphy*. We can also present a corresponding triad of temperaments, the components of which Sheldon called *viscerotonia*, *somatotonia* and *cerebrotonia*. Temperament is generally related to somatotype though the relationship is not always exact.

The four castes of Manu, *brahmin*, *kshatriya*, *vaishya*, *shudra*, are based on essence characteristics, and more or less determine the role a person plays in life. The *brahmin* is concerned with the search for truth. The *kshatriya* is a warrior or administrator and is concerned with power. The *vaishya* is a merchant or businessman concerned with making money. The *shudra* is without much inner motivation and is dependent on the other castes for employment and direction.

The ancient tetrad that relates temperament to the so called humors, *sanguinic*, *phlegmatic*, *choleric* and *melancholic*, has relevance despite the fact that the theory of the four humors was totally inaccurate. A modern version of the theory states that the overall biochemistry of people varies and that their inner chemistry determines whether they are sanguinic, choleric, phlegmatic or melancholic.

The extrovert-introvert dyad is another component of the essence. It is closely related to the somatotype. High endomorphs are almost always extroverts, high ectomorphs are usually introverts.

Know your own essence.

This involves knowing the personal laws from

which we cannot escape. Attempts to escape from them are useless and merely damage the organism.

The laws imposed by the *persona* are quite different from those imposed by the essence. *Persona* laws are not necessary and are often harmful. An example of these laws is fashion. Fashion is entirely *persona* created. It can range from the Hindu practice of demanding that widows burn themselves on the funeral pyres of their husbands to the current American practice of snorting cocaine. In the name of fashion, women in the past squeezed their guts out of place with tight corsets. In the name of fashion, women of today mutilate their feet with high-heeled shoes. It is fashion that imposes the phony quality that characterizes so much of modern art.

Its slavery to fashion demonstrates the almost infinite capacity for suggestibility that characterizes the human animal. Fashion entangles millions of humans in harmful or futile activities. Fashion is a poisonous product of the *persona*, a jungle of falsehoods in which many lose their way.

Anyone who has entered the real Work can distinguish the laws imposed by the *persona* from those imposed by the essence. The *persona* typically wants to show off. It feeds on admiration and approval. It feels compelled to follow the dictates of the social set in which it happens to move. It will do anything that is considered smart by the members of this set, whether this consists in poisoning oneself with cocaine or squeezing one's feet into impossible shoes.

It should not be concluded from the above that essence is all good and *persona* all bad. The relationship between essence and personality (to use the more general term) is not simple. Essence is what we are born with; personality is what we acquire. But suppose we have a weak essence, a defective essence, a criminal essence... Is there such a thing as a criminal essence? The annals of human crime suggest that there is. Indeed there are all sorts of essence defects which produce patterns of behavior that are not at all helpful or desirable.

So we confront a difficult question. Is it really possible to "reprogram the human biocomputer" (to borrow a phrase from neurophysiologist John Lilly)? Can we modify our own essence? If so, who in us will do the modifying? We put our faith, if we are "in the Work", in a character we call the Observer or Deputy Steward. Is this entity part of the essence or is it formed in the personality? Is it inborn or acquired?

The answer seems to be that it is both. The spiritual hunger that leads a man or woman to seek out and try to enter the Work is probably in essence. But the Seeker who gathers material about the Work and sets out to find a guide is probably in personality. In the struggle which follows to transform a slave into a master both personality and essence are involved.

Personality is not all false. It is a mixture. The false part, best described by the term *false ego*, is the major obstacle in the way of those trying to become liberated. But the genuine part of personality is capable of learning and can, by its influence, sometimes modify essence defects that would otherwise prove to be insuperable obstacles in the Way.

Correction of essence defects is always difficult. It requires great sincerity linked with equally great determination. Alcoholics, for example, may be victims of an essence defect that makes it impossible for them to take alcohol in moderation. Their situation is hopeless unless they first face facts and then resolve never to take alcohol under any circumstances. The entity that makes this decision is in personality. It can be greatly strengthened if the alcoholic associates with others who are facing a similar problem. When the new element in the personality becomes well established it begins to enter the essence. The pattern of refusing alcohol becomes, as is said, "second nature". This term "second nature" refers to patterns of behavior that started in personality and finally became part of essence.

Limiting Activities

Those who have entered the real Work will understand the importance of limiting their activities. This aspect of the Work is referred to in the aphorism:

Do only what is necessary.

Another formulation of this aphorism is:

Avoid needless karma.

The word karma refers not only to action but also to the fruits of action. Every action produces a chain of results. Some of these chains may be very long and drastically affect a person's life. A hasty decision, a few words spoken in anger, an unwise financial transaction, a chance meeting, a brief sexual encounter, all can have life-damaging consequences. We are all, to some extent, at the mercy of accidents. Those who have entered the real Work know this and they move with care. They understand the meaning of the aphorism:

Strive to live under as few laws as possible.

Random activity which is not connected with the attainment of our inner aim puts us under more laws. Above all, it puts us under the law of accident. Some people live entirely under this law. They have no inner direction, but wander here, there and everywhere impelled by chance impulses or desires. This random activity is dangerous not only because it exposes the person to all sorts of accidents but also because it is a sure way of exhausting our supply of *chi*. The importance of avoiding such random activity is formulated in the aphorism:

Substitute intentional doing for accidental happening.

Essence Activity, Persona Activity

It is easy to say "Do only what is necessary", but how do we decide whether an activity is necessary or not?

This is an important question. It confronts us with the problem of how to select our activities. We cannot avoid action. In most cases we have to work for a living. But we do have a certain amount of choice as to what actions we should do and which we should avoid.

There are certain obvious questions that need to be asked by anyone who takes the Work seriously. How will a given action affect my inner work? Will it deplete or enrich me? Will it dissipate my supply of *chi* or enhance that supply?

Activities can be divided into two categories, those which involve the essence and those which involve the personality. Activities involving the essence are real, those involving the personality are artificial. Farmers, fishermen, carpenters, plumbers, engineers, physicians, nurses, scientists, all these people are engaged in activities that are essence involving. This is because they are rooted in the real world. A farmer must confront the realities involved in growing crops. A physician must confront the realities of disease. An engineer faces the problem of building a machine that has to function in a certain way. There is no room for fantasy in this kind of work. The personality may intrude and often does, but its presence is unnecessary and often harmful.

By way of contrast, public relations experts, advertisers, most politicians, lawyers, actors, religious con-artists are engaged in activities involving personality. Their activity is not rooted in reality. If the whole lot dropped dead, life would go on.

Those who have entered the real Work will prefer the real to the artificial. They have no use for fantasy. For this reason, they will try to avoid getting involved in activities based on personality. They will particularly avoid those activities of a purely social nature that have no other function than to give people a chance to show off. Social activities of this sort are very destructive of *chi* and for this reason should be avoided.

Panic Zone, Drone Zone, Control Zone

In a previous section, the inner Work was compared to such activities as rope walking or juggling. It involves skill, attention, and a kind of relaxed awareness. In short, one must learn to "keep one's cool". This involves careful training of the Horse.

One of the most dangerous tendencies of the Horse is its proneness to panic. When the Horse panics, the whole Conveyance is placed in jeopardy. Huge amounts of emotional energy are poured out in situations that do not call for emotion at all. The emotion tends to make a dangerous or difficult situation worse.

How does one train the Horse not to panic? How does one prevent emotions from interfering with what should be purely rational decisions? How does one keep one's balance when everything seems to be conspiring to throw one off balance?

One does it by learning to enter the C zone.

What is the C zone?

The C zone is an idea developed by psychologists Robert Kriegel and Marilyn Harris Kriegel. (48) To understand it, one must first understand what is meant by the A zone and the B zone.

The A zone is a psychological territory that is more or less permanently occupied by type A people. Type A's are energetic, domineering, impatient, ambitious, tense. They are "hyped up", overactive. They undertake too much. As a result, they live in a more or less chronic state of panic and have a tendency to develop ulcers. The Kriegel's other name for the A zone is the Panic Zone.

Type B people are the opposite of A's. They are lethargic, sluggish, bored, lacking in ambition. Whereas the overmotivated A type characteristically screams "I gotta!", the undermotivated B flabbily gasps "I can't". The Kriegel's other name for the B zone is the Drone Zone.

A society dominated by type A's is hyperactive, dynamic, innovative, and more or less chronically manic. A society dominated by B's is lethargic, dull, sedate. In such a society, any innovation is regarded with suspicion, so nothing much changes.

Both A types and B types are products of their heredity. They are programmed. Their behavioral characteristics are in the essence. But the more extreme manifestations of both these kinds of behavior can be modified. Indeed, they must be modified if a balanced life-style is to be attained. Both A's and B's can develop this balanced life-style if they can learn to move into the C zone.

The characteristic of the C zone is control. This means, above all, the control of the Horse. Whereas the Horse of type A lives always on the verge of panic, the Horse of type B lies down and refuses to move. If the Conveyance is to reach the C zone, the Driver must learn to communicate with the Horse and convince that troublesome beast that neither panicking nor lying down in the road are worthy patterns of behavior. This means that the Driver, who is commonly either asleep or drunk, must at least become somewhat more awake. Who awakens the Driver? This is the task of the Observer, forerunner of the Master. How does he do it? By convincing the Driver that the awakened state is desirable.

In the C zone, there is neither the feverish "I gotta!" of the A's nor the querulous "I can't" of the B's. Life in the C zone is characterized by three C's, controlled, calm, collected. In the C zone there is a willingness to take risks and accept challenges but this willingness is moderated by an understanding of personal limitations. People who have learned to live in the C zone do not suffer from the Super-effort Syndrome. They avoid biting off more than they can chew. They do not kill themselves trying to scale Mount Everest. They know their limitations.

Life in the C zone is energized, focused and calm. Decisions are made cooly. There is neither panic nor lethargy. The athlete in the C zone, for example, balances between trying too hard and not trying hard enough, between excessive tension and over relaxation.

Above all, the quality of life in the C zone is pleasant. There is a playful quality about it. Life is fun, a game. Those in the Work who have learned how to enter the C zone realize that there is no need to sweat and grunt as one painfully tries to remember oneself. Life in the C zone leads naturally to self-remembering because it involves an element of intentional balance. This state of balance feels so good that it tends to reinforce itself. This applies to the Work in general. It is the chief reason why people persist in the Work. Certainly it involves effort, but the effort brings rewards that make it well worth while.

Seeing Triads

The real world is a world of matter and energy but the interplay of these two is hidden from us by the fog of dreams in which we spend most of our time. Learning to see this play of forces is part of our struggle to enter the real world. Hence the aphorism:

In all actions strive to see the play of the three forces.

The three forces are (1) the Force Affirming, (2) the Force Denying, (3) the Force Reconciling. It is the balance of these forces that determines whether a given activity gives us the results we desire. To get results using the wrong triad is impossible.

Triads can be destructive or creative. Creative triads produce higher levels of order. Destructive triads produce more disorder. Creative triads are difficult. Destructive triads are easy and go by themselves.

This difference can be illustrated by comparing the forces involved in building a house and burning a house. Striking one match may be all the effort it takes to burn a house. To rebuild that house, time, effort and skill are all required. Skill is essential. Effort embodies the Force Affirming, but skill embodies the Force Reconciling, or Third Force. If the builder lacks the necessary skill, the house will not be built correctly no matter how much effort he puts into the work.

The more difficult the triad the more significant is the role of the Third Force. Consider three examples. I start with the trunk of a tree. I wish to convert it into firewood. This is an easy triad. Anyone able to wield a saw and a splitting maul can do it. Next, I decide to carve a bowl or a spoon from some of the wood. This requires more skill. It also requires different tools, for tools are the transmitters of the Third Force. Without the right tools the craftsman cannot exert the Third Force no matter how great his skill. Next, suppose I decide to carve some of the wood into a statue. This requires more skill than it takes to carve a bowl or spoon. It involves a different triad.

We can classify triads on the basis of the amount of effort and skill they demand. A purely destructive triad, such as the one involved in burning a house, demands neither skill nor effort. A selectively destructive triad such as dismantling a house so that the wood, bricks, windows, and doors may be re-used requires more effort. Building a completely new house calls for still more effort. Inventing an entirely new type of house would call for the use of a different triad, the triad of invention. This triad is also involved in scientific research and artistic creation.

The high creative triads are all difficult and only a relatively few people are able to use them. This applies particularly to the triad of the inner Work. It is a skilled activity. The special form of skill involved in the Work is described by the Sanskrit word *upaya*. It is generally translated as "skillful means". The triad of the inner Work does not call for the kind of heavy labor involved in digging a ditch or splitting firewood. It calls for relaxed awareness and balance like that displayed by the skillful juggler or tightrope walker. Those who work on themselves as if they were trying to split a log by brute force are victims of the Super-effort Syndrome and liable to do themselves more harm than good.

Seeing Alchemically

Among the powers which those in the real Work must strive to develop is the ability to *see* alchemically. This is a special faculty for which there is no word in English. Clairvoyance, which really means clear seeing, could be used, but the word carries certain associations which make it unsuitable.

Seeing alchemically involves the direct perception of changes in materiality brought about by the action of triads. The concept of different levels of materiality is one of those items which form part of the special system of knowledge on which the real Work is based. Creative activity endows material with a higher level of materiality. This can only be perceived by those who have learned to *see* alchemically. A bowl or spoon carved from a log of wood has a higher level than the log from which it came. A statue, if skillfully carved by a gifted artist, has a still higher level.

Works of real objective art have a very high level of materiality. They produce strong psychological effects on those capable of absorbing the impressions they transmit. The spiritual level of a civilization can be measured by the amount of objective art it generates. By this criterion, our technological civilization is not much better than a gadget-infested barbarism.

Alchemy is chemistry taken beyond the limits recognized by the chemist. Alchemists perceive their own bodies as alembics designed by Nature for the transmutation of materials. They know that, in the state of hypnotized sleep in which we pass most of our time, the transmutation of materials stops short. It could go a lot further but it does not. This is because the vital transforming agent, *chi*, is dissipated in useless or harmful activities.

The Work is an act of self-creation and the triad involved is analogous to the one employed in the production of objective art. It involves the production of a higher form of being. This involves two acts of creation, the formation of the Observer and the transformation of the Observer into the Master. The Master is, in fact, already within us, but we have no contact with this entity because we live in the lowest part of our inner dwelling.

What Is the Master?

That entity we call the Master has two aspects, the *Master in the Body* and the *Master beyond the Body*.

The Master in the Body is located in the organizer. The organizer is the seat of what has been called "the wisdom of the body". It comes into existence at that moment when the nucleus of the sperm fuses with the nucleus of the ovum. This act of fusion marks the beginning of a new life. Birth is not the beginning of the new life. Nuclear fusion is the beginning.

The organizer creates a morphogenetic field about the fertilized egg. The great multitude of cells which arise from this egg are guided and differentiated by this field. During the first phase of life, which takes place in the uterus and lasts nine months, biological time is stretched to permit the accomplishment of an enormous feat of bioengineering. This involves the formation not only of the fetus with all its organs but also of the placenta which burrows into the walls of the uterus to feed the fetus. At the end of nine months the placenta is already senile and starting to decay. The fetus, on the other hand, has only just started its existence. It emerges into the light, emitting a howl of horror and amazement, and can expect to live as long as a hundred years. Its companion, the placenta, is unceremoniously dumped in the garbage.

The organizer, which oversees this feat of creation, is not located in any one organ. It pervades the organism as a whole and gives it form. Every organism must have an organizer. Without it, the cell mass would be shapeless, a cancer-like blob.

Within the organizer there is a timer. This timer determines the life span of the organism. Among mammals the life span varies enormously. Man has a longer life span than most mammals, one hundred years if he takes proper care of his body. This long span is divided into four phases.

Phase I. *Fetal* phase. Duration nine months. In this phase all the main organ systems are shaped by the organizer.

Phase II. *Childhood*. Duration about eighteen years. The prolongation of phase II is characteristic of Man. Whereas most mammals mature in a year, he takes eighteen, and is not very mature even then. During phase II, the growth of the body continues. At puberty, the timer in the organizer switches on the sex organs, flooding the organism with the hormones involved in sexual arousal. Unfortunately, for the peace of mind of their possessors, the sex organs mature before the boy or girl matures and greatly increase the storm and stress of adolescence.

Phase III. *Householder*. Duration about thirty years. In this phase the normal man and woman combine forces to produce children and to raise the children until they reach responsible age.

Phase IV. *Sannyasin*. Duration variable. In this phase, in a spiritually mature society, both men and women devote themselves to the completion of their inner Work in order that, at death, they may be able to blend consciously with the force that gave them life. Needless to say, our society is anything but spiritually mature and the lives of most elderly people are wasted in futility.

Throughout these phases the organizer holds the body together and supervises its inevitable aging. The organizer runs the show though the ego knows nothing about it. The ego is, in fact, a very minor component of the whole. It perches like a seagull on the iceberg which is nine tenths submerged below the water. It is the organizer that manages the inner economy. It sees to the repair of the body which is constantly wearing out. It replaces lost cells, heals injuries, sees to the transformation of food into flesh. It maintains the vital balance which is essential for the body's survival.

Our personal organizer is an atom of the Great Organizer, a manifestation of the Mind Force and the Life Force. It was these two forces that generated Earth's biosphere in the first place and directed the course of organic evolution. The Great Organizer is another name for the Old One, the God of the *creatura*. It created the entire hierarchy of the megalocosmos and all the beings it contains. It is, at this point in the flow of time, about fifteen billion years old.

All this has a direct bearing on the work of transforming the Observer into the Master. The Master is already there. We do not have to create it. It is part of the organizer and it pervades the body as its field of force pervades a magnet. The ego, prancing around and playing its silly little games, is quite unaware of this field of force. It calls itself "I" and attributes to itself will. In fact it has neither I nor will. It is merely a helpless puppet. (49)

UNIVERSAL MANDALA

The Courts of the Mandala

Those who have really entered the Work are concerned with more serious matters than the prancing and posturings of their personal egos. They have begun to be directly aware of the mysterious field of force that organizes their being. They are receiving the wisdom of the Old One which generated life on Earth in the first place and has, after three and a half billion years, produced a creature that calls itself *Homo sapiens.*

This direct awareness of the wisdom of the Old One results from the discovery of the Master. Those that have accomplished this feat can *see* directly into the nature of things. They are able to see the morphogenetic fields that hold all organisms together and to understand how those fields overlap and interact. As the mystic, Jacob Boehme, put it, they can see "the signatures of all things". This ability to see enables them to understand the fate of all things and the place each organism occupies in the Chain of Being.

In the Universal Mandala there are two courts, the *Court of the Creatura* and the *Court of the Hidden Powers.* Those who have learned to read the signature of all things have entered the outer court, the *Court of the Creatura .* Entering this court is no easy matter. It involves overcoming the guardians at the four gates which, in this context, stand for the four functions, instinctive, moving, emotional and intellectual. Only one who has brought about the harmonious interaction of all four functions can pass the guardians.

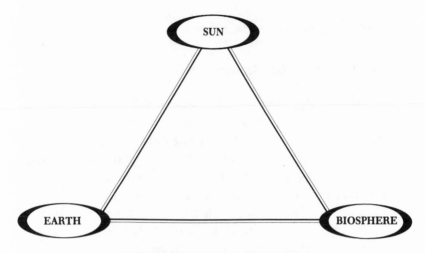

TRIAD OF THE MACROCOSM

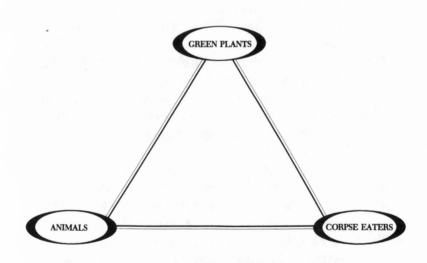

TRIAD OF THE BIOSPHERE

DIAGRAM OF FATE

There is much to be learned in the *Court of the Creatura*. It provides those who have entered the court with the key to the nature of life on this planet. Life is a product of the great triad, Sun-Earth-Biosphere. The active force comes from the Sun, the passive force from the Earth and the biosphere in its entirety represents the third force. Within the biosphere are a multitude of secondary triads. The chief of these consists of green plants that feed on sunlight, animals that feed on plants and decay organisms that recycle the bodies both of plants and animals.

The triad Sun-Earth-Biosphere is the macrocosm for Man. He exists within it. He depends on it for the food he eats, the air he breathes and almost all the impressions he receives through his senses. The macrocosm imposes on him a set of laws, all of which are inescapable. On a large scale the macrocosm determines his fate. Any major derangement of the macrocosm could destroy him. He is quite capable, being stupid and deeply asleep, of bringing about such a major derangement himself. This he could do either by starting a thermonuclear war or by completely destroying the tropical rain forests. He could add to this damage pouring into the atmosphere vast quantities of carbon dioxide generated by his frenzied consumption of various fossil fuels.

All this is conventional knowledge available to anyone, but those who enter the *Court of the Creatura* have a great deal more than this conventional knowledge. Entry into this court confers upon the initiate the powers inherent in what has been called King Solomon's Ring. Tradition tells us that Solomon had the power to converse with the beasts, the birds and the plants. This he could do by entering into the aura of any entity with which he wished to communicate.

The aura contains the essence of the creature. Those who can enter the aura transform themselves for a while into the organism with which the aura is associated. This ability to enter the aura of another creature is part of the equipment of the shaman who uses it to draw power from the animal with which he or she communicates. The shaman *becomes* the animal and uses its power for his own purposes.

In his stimulating book on neo-shamanism, E.J. Gold has detailed methods that may be used in what he calls "voyaging in the labyrinth". (50) Gold's labyrinth is the *Court of the Creatura*, the "macrodimensional maze of living electrical force" that is diffused throughout the Earth's biosphere. This is the force that manifests itself in every living organism through its morphogenetic field or aura.

A word of caution, however, needs to be offered to those who would venture into this macro-dimensional maze. It is difficult to distinguish between real and imaginary experiences. The practice of "life extending shapeshifting", which means entering the aura of another being so thoroughly that one feels one *is* that being, involves extending *chi*. In order to extend *chi* one must have *chi*. For this particular operation one needs a lot of it.

The real shaman (and there are phony shamans in plenty) generates *chi* by the struggle between yes and no. This generally involves a number of physical ordeals designed both to toughen the body and strengthen the will. The training of the real shaman is extremely tough. It is not a career to be entered upon lightly.

What happens to those who try to enter the *Court of the Creatura* without the necessary power? Generally nothing. They just indulge in games of "let's pretend". Children are always playing such games. "Let's pretend I'm a bear. Let's pretend I'm a snake." They growl, they hiss. Such games may be fun but they have absolutely nothing to do with shamanism. They are merely one more example of the fantasy Work.

Beyond the *Court of the Creatura* lies the *Court of the Hidden Powers*. This court is harder to enter than is the *Court of the Creatura*. The guardians at the gates into this court are ferocious. Those who blunder into this court without proper preparation are apt to lose their sanity. This was what happened to Friedrich Nietzsche. He saw too much. C.G. Jung also entered this court but managed to keep his sanity. He described his experience in *Memories, Dreams, Reflections* in the chapter entitled "Confrontation with the Unconscious".

The powers which are encountered in the *Court of the Hidden Powers* have been called the Fates. The poet Goethe, who knew how to enter this court, called them the Mothers. He realized that entering this court involved danger. "Now let me dare to open wide the gate/ Past which men's steps have ever flinching trod." He called the hidden forces the Mothers because they give shape to the body of events. They are the hidden forces which determine the course of life on Earth. They regulate the process of organic evolution which is not the result of blind accident as the Darwinians imagine.

So what have the Mothers in store for Earth's problem child, *Homo sapiens*? Those who have entered the *Court of the Hidden Powers* can answer this question but they are not talking. All they will say is that the fate of *Homo sapiens* is in the balance. He has broken many laws, learned things he had no right to know, released forces that should never have been released. His future now depends on whether he has enough intelligence to correct his mistakes. If he does not correct them, he will be wiped out as surely as were the Dodo and the Passenger Pigeon.

The adepts who understand the forces that shape Man's fate can do nothing to change that fate. They see contemporary humanity as a crowd of careless children playing near the ocean. The children are very busy. They are building sand castles, gathering pretty pebbles and shells, fighting over who shall have the most pebbles.

Meanwhile, far out at sea, large forces are at work, forces about which the children know nothing. Those forces are generating mighty waves which will hit the beach with devastating impact, wiping out the sand castles, scattering the children's shells and pebbles, drowning huge numbers of the children themselves.

Should the adepts who have this knowledge warn the children? What good would that do? The children are not listening. They are far too busy to look out to sea. They want more shells, more pebbles, bigger sand castles. The last thing they wish to hear is that their activities are futile and that their very lives are in danger. So the adepts say nothing.

Beyond the Creatura

Beyond the *Court of the Hidden Powers*, at the very center of the Mandala, is the monad, the world beyond creation. It cannot be described because it has no specific qualities. It is a void which contains all possibilities. The Gnostics called it the *pleroma*, the fullness, and contrasted it with the *creatura*, the world in which possibilities are realized. The *pleroma* is timeless, spaceless, devoid of attributes, the Eternal Unchanging. It contains in potential an infinite number of universes. We exist in one such universe. There may be many others existing parallel with ours. We cannot enter them because each universe has its own space time framework.

The *pleroma* is the seed, the *bindu*. All worlds emerge from it. All return to it. The *pleroma* is the God-outside-creation, the unmanifested Brahma, the "Unknown One".

Through the *Master beyond the Body* we can blend into the *pleroma*. This represents for Man the ultimate stage of the spiritual journey. Such a one has climbed the highest peak of the Mountain of Liberation and vanished at the top, blending into what is sometimes called "the clear light of the void". Many people, it is said, experience the clear light at the moment of death, but one who has

completed his inner development enters the light
before he sheds his body. In one part of his being he
is outside spacetime. He has put into practice the
aphorism:

*Learn to stand on the bank of time's river and
watch the flow.*

Esoteric Schools

One thing is certain. The "Great Society" is
indifferent to the Work. It does not even recognize
its existence. So the question arises: Can those who
do value the Work create intentional communities
in which the Work can be practiced without the
distractions provided by a materialistic society?

Intentional communities can indeed be created
and have been at various times and in various
places. These are the so-called esoteric schools. They
exist to teach the methods of self-transcendence both
to the adults and to the children who belong to
them. How effectively they manage to do this
depends entirely on the level of development of the
people who run the school.

A school can operate correctly only if the person
in charge is a Master. This means that he or she has
climbed at least part of the way up the Mountain of
Liberation, is free of the urge to play ego games, is a
servant of the Work and a servant of truth. Only one
who has reached this level of development can safely
undertake such a difficult enterprise.

People at this high level of development are rare.
Moreover, those who have reached this level may

not feel much inclined to start a school. They are likely to have in mind the aphorism which states:

The itch to teach others is often a manifestation of ego.

This aphorism is very true. Phony teachers and phony schools greatly outnumber the real ones. Such schools trap large numbers of seekers, especially young people who lack discrimination. Membership in such a phony school can seriously damage the psyches of young people. It can bring their search for a real teacher to an end and permanently turn them against the Work.

It may be said that this is only what they deserve for having plunged carelessly into a dangerous region. An aphorism states that the pupil always gets the teacher he or she deserves.

A fool gets a fool for a teacher, a fraud gets a fraud.

This is true. There is no sentimentality in the Work. Those who set out on the Way do so at their peril. Having broken out of the Treadmill they must find their way through the Forest. The Forest is full of traps, of paths that lead nowhere and of guides that do not know the way. To avoid falling into the traps the seeker needs a goodly supply of the three sacred qualities, *practicality, determination* and *discrimination,* particularly the latter.

Phony esoteric schools entice new members with all sorts of alluring prospects. They will equip their members with mysterious psychic powers, prolong their lives, strengthen their wills, enlarge their incomes, enhance their sexual prowess and even teach them how to fly! There is no limit to the goodies they offer.

Such enticements should, by themselves, serve as a warning to the seeker. A genuine esoteric school does not advertise. Far from trying to attract new members, it tends to discourage applicants. The difficulties and dangers of the Way are emphasized. It is better not to start at all than to start and then give up. It is better to remain comfortably asleep than to become half awake.

Those who are admitted to the school as neophytes are given every opportunity to leave it. The Master, far from offering encouragement, is apt to ignore the beginner. He finds fault with practically everything that the newcomer does. He tests the neophyte's level of determination and discrimination by placing all sorts of obstacles in his way. He lets the seeker know that the Work is not for weaklings, nor is it for fools. It is a form of spiritual athletics equivalent to competing in the Olympic games. Those who are not ready to train intensively should avoid the Work and try something easier.(51)

Another sign of the quality of a school is its size. Phony schools tend to be very big. Phony Masters, being ego dominated, set no limit to the number of their pupils. They open branches of the school all over the place and rake in large sums in dues from their numerous followers. It is not unusual for such phony Masters to number their disciples in thousands. On most of those followers they have not even set eyes.

A genuine Master behaves very differently. He knows that a real school is based on the *halka*, the circle. The *halka* resembles a wheel. The Master is at the center. His closest pupils form a ring about him and he is connected to each of them as the rim of a wheel is connected to the hub by its spokes. The Master and pupils together constitute a Ring of Power. Together they can generate more power than can any of the individuals who make up the circle.

Halkas are governed by strict rules. For example, it is absolutely forbidden for any member of the circle to reveal to outsiders what goes on in the group. This rule of silence is essential for the protection of the members who may, in the course of meeting, learn various things about each other which could be damaging if generally known. The rule of silence also puts a restraint on that habit of needless talk, so characteristic of our usual sleepy state.

The *halka* can never be a large group. Generally it consists of twelve members, including the Master. If it gets much bigger than this, the rapport between pupils and Master breaks down.

The *halka* functions as the heart and brain of the intentional community. All major decisions relating to the community are made by the members of the *halka*. These members constitute the all important core group, without which the community will fall apart.

Though small, the *halka* spreads out its influence quite widely. This is because most of its members have groups of their own. By running such groups they gain useful experience. This activity is a part of the real Work, a form of paying one's dues. What one has received one must hand on, or try to, always realizing that there is a limit to the amount people can receive. In this connection, members of the *halka* are advised to bear in mind that saying of popular wisdom which states, *You can lead a horse to water but you cannot make it drink.*

In all esoteric schools there is a tendency for the core group to suffer from elitism. The pupils nearest the Master think of themselves as the elect. It is exactly this tendency that a genuine Master will oppose most vigorously. Having outgrown ego trips himself he will do his best to prevent his pupils from falling into this trap.

A real Master sees himself as a servant of the Work and a servant of truth. He is not out to impress people, to dominate others or to accumulate wealth. Certainly he has the power to dominate others. He would not be a Master if he lacked this power. He is able to resist the temptation to use the power for his own aggrandizement. He regards his power not as a personal possession but as a gift from the Mind Force that created him in the first place. To any members of his inner circle who are beginning to develop power and showing signs of throwing their weight about he will offer the same advice as did Jesus when his disciples started arguing about who was greatest.

Whosoever would be greatest let him be as a servant among you.

Blind Spots and Buffers

The work of a teacher in an esoteric school has two aspects. He tries to create conditions that are favorable to the real Work, and he holds up a mirror in which those who wish to see can see. He cannot force anyone to look into that mirror. In the real Work there can be no coercion. No one can be forced to see what they don't want to see.

This is a law of the Work. Violent methods are ruled out. Such methods are used only by those teachers who incline toward what is picturesquely known as the left hand path.(52)

A teacher confronts endless resistance. The students often appear to be both blind and deaf. They wish to be told only what they like to hear. They perfectly exemplify what one Sufi Master has called "The Motto of the Human Race":

Tell me what to do; but it must be what I want you to tell me. (53)

Why is it so difficult to get students to see those aspects of themselves that stand in the way of their progress towards inner freedom?

To answer this question we must study the force that keeps the blindfolded slaves in the Treadmill from recognizing their slavery. The Overseer of the Treadmill, a master of deception, manages to introduce into the psyches of the slaves mechanisms called blind spots or buffers. (54) These buffers are designed to prevent violent collisions between contradictory aspects of the collection of petty selves that together constitute the ego. Buffers are very powerful and very necessary. If the slaves want to be happy in their slavery (most of them do) they must have buffers. It is only when the slaves escape from the Treadmill and try to find their way to freedom that buffers become obstacles.

Unfortunately those who leave the Treadmill to wander in the Forest take their buffers with them. The Observer in such people, whose job it is to see who is who in the zoo, is constantly frustrated by the buffers. They conceal just those features of the ego that must be seen if any real progress is to be made.

Buffers fall into a number of categories but all have one thing in common. They enable people to continue lying to themselves even as they proclaim that their main preoccupation is to find the truth.

Two categories of buffers often develop in people who imagine they are in the Work. They are called the Tramp and the Zealot. They exert their effects through very different mechanisms.

The Tramp lacks any permanent abode. He drifts. He lacks the ability to fulfil obligations. Many people who believe they have entered the Work have a Tramp aboard their personal Ship of Fools. The Tramp prevents them from making any real progress.

A skilled teacher sees this. He will ask such a person to promise to perform some task that will bring him or her face to face with the Tramp. In the struggle which ensues the task will either not be performed at all or performed very badly. There will be endless excuses and explanations. "I couldn't do it because, because and because..." The teacher will listen. Perhaps he will say nothing. Perhaps he will advise the student to be more careful when making promises, quoting the afore-mentioned Sufi Master.

Never promise, even by implication, without fulfilling your promise.

The only acceptable alternative to completing an undertaking is to over-fulfil it.

To betray any promise, explicit or otherwise, will harm you more than it can harm anyone else. (55)

The Tramp makes promises casually because he has no permanent standards. He shifts around, changes with every wind, is here today and somewhere else tomorrow. The Tramp buffer system makes it hard for those afflicted with it ever to face the real source of their weakness. They feel no remorse of conscience about broken promises. They probably do not even notice that they have broken them. Sooner or later even the most patient teacher will tell the Tramp-dominated student to go elsewhere. Such people are unteachable.

The Tramp-dominated student harms only himself. The same cannot be said of the student whose buffer system centers around the Zealot. Zealot-dominated students are the opposite of Tramps. They commonly over-perform the tasks assigned them, bringing to their work a fanatical enthusiasm. It is exactly this fanatical enthusiasm that makes them dangerous. They go to extremes. They suffer chronically from the super-effort syndrome. They are type A's who drive themselves hard and struggle to impose their views on everyone else.

Zealots, though they appear to be devoted to the teacher, never allow that teacher to interfere with their fanatical beliefs or shake their confidence in the correctness of their own views. They will distort the teachings in the most astonishing ways and all the time insist that they are following the teacher's "hidden instructions". They make a big deal out of those "hidden instructions", insisting that they alone have understood the teacher's words.

For the conscientious teacher the Zealot represents a difficult problem. It is best, of course, never to let Zealots into the group because a buffer system centering around the Zealot is almost impossible to break down. But it is hard to tell just how unbalanced a Zealot is. His or her enthusiasm about the Work (and Zealots are always passionately enthusiastic) may easily deceive the teacher. Confronted, as he usually is, by lukewarm weaklings whose half-hearted efforts will never produce any real results, a teacher is apt to welcome anyone in whom the fire of passion seems to burn. Unfortunately, in the Zealot, the fire of passion burns out of control.

After the death of a teacher it is the Zealots among his students who tend to take charge. The Zealot's fanatical intensity, his unshakable belief in the correctness of his own opinions, his conviction that he alone understands the teacher's "secret message", gives him the power to dominate his less aggressive fellows.

This domination by Zealots was clearly demonstrated during the early days of the Christian church. By the 3rd century A.D. the Zealots had already turned the original teachings upside down and enclosed them behind a wall of dogmas that no "true believer" was allowed to question. As soon as they had physical power the Zealots engaged in those heresy hunts which did so much to sully the reputation of the church. With the very best intentions (Zealots always have good intentions) they converted a teaching centering around love to one permeated with intolerance, violence and hate.

The Tramp and the Zealot are just two of the psychological mechanisms through which buffer systems operate. There are many others. One of the functions of an effective group is to help its members see their blind spots. The buffers, though invisible to their possessors, are often quite obvious to other members of the group as well as to the teacher. But the study of buffers demands a high level of sincerity on the part of members of the group, a willingness to confront reality and not to take refuge in fantasy. Such a willingness is rare. More often group members waste their time in the exchange of platitudes about the Work, in useless speculations, amiable chit-chat, wooly theorizings and the generation of large volumes of mystical hot air. Such groups do more harm than good to their members.

Building an Ark

Now I return in memory to that foggy winter afternoon in 1936 when I finally accepted P.D. Ouspensky as my teacher. We were walking round the farm at Lyne Place in England discussing the problem of self-sufficiency. In the year 1936 war

was already on the horizon. Ouspensky thought that
the struggle would be long and hard and that it
might   prove   disastrous   for   our   weakened
civilization. If we were to survive we must begin to
prepare.

"It is necessary to build an ark," said Ouspensky.
"One must start building now, not wait for the flood
to begin."

The Biblical story of the great flood had special
significance for Ouspensky. For him it was an
allegory and referred to the fall of civilization. Such
a fall, he declared, would be accompanied by the
annihilation of the greater part of the human race.
This   would   result   from   geological   upheavals,
epidemics, revolutions, mass migrations. (He wrote
before the invention of thermonuclear devices, or
would probably have put them at the head of the
list.)

The most significant part of the allegory was the
building of the ark. By means of the ark, carefully
prepared before hand by people of wisdom, the
most important ideas and attainments of a given
culture would be saved from destruction. The ark,
explained Ouspensky, represented the esoteric
school in which certain people could be prepared to
make the transition to a higher form of life, a new
birth. The ark represented the "inner circle of
humanity".

The allegory of the ark has another meaning
which has special significance for us today. God
made Noah responsible for the lives of all creatures,
as is clearly stated in the sixth chapter of Genesis.

*And of every living thing of all flesh, two of every
sort shalt thou bring into the ark, to keep them alive
with thee; they shall be male and female.*

*Of fowls after their kind, and of cattle after their
kind, of every creeping thing of the earth after his
kind, two of every sort shall come unto thee, to keep
them alive.*

*And take thou unto thee all food that is eaten, and
thou shalt gather it to thee, and it shall be for food
for thee and for them.*

*Thus did Noah. According to all that God
commanded him so he did.* (56)

Noah was the first conservationist. He was made
responsible for the survival of creatures other than
the members of his immediate family. In Noah we
see the first example of Man in the role of protector
of life on Earth.

Today we have managed, by the misapplication
of our technology, to place ourselves in the opposite
role to that of Noah. Modern Man has become the
destroyer of life on Earth. Fortunately his transition
from life-protector to life-destroyer has not passed
unnoticed. In quite a large number of people, it has
served to awaken a new kind of awareness. They
have seen pictures of the planet Earth taken from
space. They have become conscious of its unique
quality, the only planet in our solar system that has
a mantle of living things. They have also become
aware of the fact that, in the great mosaic of living
things on the planet's surface, all the ecosystems
interact. If you damage one you will affect the
others.

It is for this reason that the building of the ark constitutes a meaningful activity for those able, like Noah, to understand the realities of the situation. We are threatened today, not so much by a natural disaster, as by the results of our own greed and lack of foresight. The builders of contemporary arks must be true to what one might call "the Noah tradition". They must see themselves in the role of life-protectors. They must be conscious of a sacred trust, of a special responsibility imposed on Man. They must be aware of the interdependence of living things and see themselves as only one link in the chain of being. They must be realists, not romantics. They must understand that, if we damage Earth's biosphere, our own life support systems will suffer. It may be within our power to pull down the temple of life but, if we do so, we shall perish in the ruins.

The task of building an ark can provide a focus both for the outer and the inner Work. Building the external ark is only half of the operation. Building the inner ark is just as important. It is this inner ark that gives to its possessor the capacity to remain separated from external events and not to be overwhelmed either by what passes for success or by what seems to be failure.

A contemporary ark must be based on the idea of an ecologically balanced community. The humans can adopt a protective attitude toward the other members of the community. They have to realize, however, that there is an absolute limit to the number of plants and animals that a given area of land can maintain. This number is determined by the fertility of the soil, the amount of rain, the hours of sunshine, average temperature, the nature of the covering vegetation. Humans, in order to grow the crops they need, will have to modify that vegetation, but they will avoid drastic interference with the established ecosystems and introduce the changes they make gradually.

Ark building is a practical activity. It is also an educational experience. All the major divisions of science, physics, chemistry and biology, can be studied directly. The transformations involved in the various food chains all demonstrate laws. Photons from the sun, trapped by the chlorophyll of green leaves, are built into complex molecules in a series of steps. These molecules, in the form of proteins, fats, carbohydrates, vitamins, provide all the raw materials needed by the vegetarian members of the food chain. As for the carnivores, they get their raw materials by killing and eating the vegetarians.

For its human members, building the ark can be the supreme educational experience. In our society the whole idea of education has been misunderstood. First, it is thought of as being needed only during a person's youth. Second, it is equated with the acquisition of special knowledge that will enable a person to earn a living. The end product of this kind of education is a certificate to be hung on a wall, stating that its possessor is trained to practice law, medicine, psychology, business administration, and so on.

This is vocational training, not real education. It produces specialists and narrows people's

awareness. It educates only the intellectual brain
and ignores the fact that we are more than our
intellects. Real education has to be designed to help
develop the whole of a person's being. It generates
an awareness that we humans are but a small part in
a large and complex whole. It is holistic.

Ark building, as an educational activity, makes
the following demands of the builders.

1. They must understand the interdependence of
   living things and develop a willingness to live
   and let live.
2. They must understand the law of limitation of
   growth. It is contrary to the law that any one
   species should grow to such an extent that it
   takes over the biosphere.
3. They must be willing to take a low place on
   the food chain. We are primates, and
   primates, on the whole, are not carnivores.
4. They must accept the fact that education has
   to be a lifelong experience.

The work of ark building, if it is done effectively,
will produce men and women who have emerged
from the narrow confines of the personal ego. Do
such people constitute what P.D. Ouspensky called
"the inner circle of humanity"? Perhaps they do, but
the term is not a good one. It carries an element of
mystery, it implies esotericism. There is nothing
esoteric about the ark builders. They are not the
guardians of some sacred mystery nor do they claim
to have higher powers. They are practical men and
women who understand the laws under which they

live. Because they understand the laws both of the microcosm and of the macrocosm, they can see what the future holds more clearly than can their fellows who do not understand these laws. They recognize the existence of certain rather obvious truths. Those who upset the balance of the biosphere must put up with the chaos that results. Those who persist in overbreeding will wreck their life support systems. Those who poison earth, air and water will be poisoned in their turn.

As with the outer laws so with the inner laws. We humans have one law imposed on us by the force that created us. If we wish to be happy, healthy and productive, we must struggle to emerge from the world of dreams and to enter the real world. In our usual state of waking sleep we have neither inner unity, inner direction nor real will. We are merely puppets pulled by invisible strings. To become free we must awaken. To be awake is everything.

The spiritual sickness of our age results from the lack of clearly defined life aims. To an increasing extent everything is being done for us. Computerized robots take over one job after another. More and more humans are becoming technologically unemployed. They can find no place in the economy. This is not good either for the body or for the soul.

The struggle to build an ark can provide a worthwhile life aim for the builders. Both the building of the inner ark and the external ark demand from the builder a combination of power and wisdom if they are to be built correctly. A properly constructed ark will contain all three vital

components, garden, temple, university, needed to
feed the three aspects of human totality. The garden
feeds the body, the temple feeds the soul and the
university the mind. Within such an ark, a man or
woman can learn both how to live rightly and how
to die rightly. One can hardly ask for more than
this.

What is Success?

An elderly American approached an even older
Sufi and complained as follows:

"As you probably know, we Americans worship
success. But we have one great problem. We
generally cannot define what we mean by success.

"Take my own life as an example. At one time I
thought that the secret of success lay in the family.
So I married a good woman and we had children.
They were good children, studied hard, did well. I
have no complaints on that score. My family life was
successful. But so what? My wife is now dead. My
children have children of their own. I have only
accomplished what any good animal does,
reproduced my kind and reared my young.

"I also thought that my career would provide the
key to success. I was a physicist. I delved into the
secrets of matter and energy. I worked as part of a
team serving a gigantic atom-smasher. We used
billions of electron volts trying to shatter protons.
That game was exciting while it lasted. Now it seems
only an exercise in futility. I see the gigantic atom-
smashers (and they are proposing to build bigger
and bigger ones) as an almost criminal waste. Surely

we can find better things to do with our brains and our money.

"I also looked for success in the realm of books. I was gifted with the ability to write clearly about subjects generally considered obscure. So I wrote. My books were published. Some of them sold, some didn't. So what? There they sit on the shelf like fossils of my former thoughts.

"So here I am, retired, a "success" by the standards most Americans apply. My name is in *Who's Who*. My books are still read. I have three children, five grandchildren, two houses, an adequate income, and I enjoy excellent health for a man of my age. And yet, I feel that I have somehow missed the boat, wasted my time, not accomplished anything. But what should I have accomplished? Can you give me the recipe for real success?"

"Willingly," said the Sufi, "but you are not likely to accept it. This recipe is not for everyone. It is contained in four very simple aphorisms."

At this point the Sufi paused, then, as if he were chanting a magical formula, he slowly and deliberately pronounced the following:

Expect nothing.
Demand nothing.
Desire nothing.
Be nothing.

He paused again, giving the message time to sink in. The American made no comment. The message was certainly not what he had expected, but, as the very first aphorism had been "expect nothing", he could hardly complain.

The Sufi chuckled.

"I told you you wouldn't like it. But you asked so I was bound to answer. In my order of Sufism, we do not teach or preach but we consider ourselves bound to answer honest questions. Your question was honest. It came from the heart, not from the head."

"I don't understand," said the American. "Especially the last of your aphorisms. "Be nothing". If I *am* nothing I might as well be dead."

"Ah," said the Sufi, "but there is more than one way of dying. We have a saying, 'die before you die'. It involves annihilation at one level and rebirth at another. The aphorisms constitute the Four Pillars of Spiritual Nihilism. On those four you can build the Tavern of Ruin. Enter the tavern. Call on Saki, the Cup Bearer, to bring you a cup of *fana*, the Wine of Annihilation. Drink deeply. As you drink meditate on these verses of our immortal Omar.

We are no other than a moving row
Of magic shadow-shapes that come and go
Round with this Sun-illumined Lantern held
In Midnight by the Master of the Show;

Impotent Pieces in the Game He plays
Upon this Chequer-board
of Nights and Days;
Hither and thither moves,
and checks, and slays,
And one by one back in the Closet lays." (57)

The American felt moved to protest.

"That is sheer determinism. If we are 'impotent pieces in the game he plays' there is nothing we can do. We play our parts because we have no choice. You seem to suggest that the whole performance is programmed in advance."

"Perhaps it is. Who knows? There is a force that creates and a force that destroys. They play a game, batting us humans back and forth between them. Call them the Light Force and the Dark Force. When the Light Force predominates we are creative and build things. Then the Dark Force predominates and we become destructive. We tear things down and start to kill each other. So periods of creativity alternate with periods of destruction. Look at the history of our twentieth century. It should have been a gloriously creative time. Instead it has seen some of the worst bouts of mass destructiveness that our unfortunate species has ever indulged in."

"Can we choose which force we serve?"

"Perhaps. It depends on our understanding. Some people know the secret of the great game. They can choose. They can consciously serve either the Light Force or the Dark Force. But those who know nothing are merely pawns in the game, pushed here and there by forces they do not see."

"Why is the secret of the game hidden from us?"

"It is not hidden. All the prophets and liberators have told the secret. It was formulated particularly clearly by the Prophet Jesus. But most people who call themselves Christians still know nothing about it. The secret was concealed long ago by the Fathers of the Church who entombed it in dogmas and rituals and fantastic myths. What happened to Christianity also happened to most of the teachings brought by the liberators. They were entombed in dogmatic religions by authoritarian priests who persuaded the gullible that they alone possessed the keys to the great mystery. Only the gnostics knew that this was a lie which is why the professional priests so hate the gnostics."

"How is it that the gnostics know the secret?"

"Who knows? They seem to have been born with it. But not all gnostics make use of their knowledge. There are theoretical gnostics and practical gnostics. The theoretical gnostics merely theorize. They discuss, debate, philosophize. They generate clouds of mystical hot air. The practical gnostics keep the talk to a minimum and get on with the job."

"So what is the job?"

"The job is to become both actor and spectator, to act in and, at the same time, to watch the play. The job is to transform a slave into a master. The job is to shed the personal ego as a snake sheds its skin and to blend with the force that gave us life and mind."

"Is this really possible?"

"Who knows? Find out for yourself. You live near the ocean. Watch the waves. Let them teach you."

"The waves?"

"Yes, indeed. What is the characteristic of ocean waves?"

"Waves form, crest, break, sweep up the beach and flow back into the ocean."

"Exactly. They die and are replaced, but the ocean remains. But suppose a wave imagined it could survive death. Suppose it fantasized about a "world to come" in which it would have "life everlasting". In that "world to come" all waves would exist forever, the "good" waves in a place called heaven, the "bad" waves in a terrible place called hell."

"That would be a pretty foolish fantasy for a wave."

"Exactly. But millions of human beings take this fantasy seriously. They want to hang on to their personal egos. They want to carry those egos with them beyond death. They don't like the idea of blending back into the ocean from which they came. But the gnostics have no use for this pathetic fantasy.

"So this is the secret of the gnostics. Now, while you still have the body, enter the Tavern of Ruin and leave your ego outside. Discover and blend with your higher Self, which is part of the Mind Force and the Life Force that created us all. This ocean of life is, for us, the *creatura*, the Creator God.

"But God is both in time and outside of time. There is God the Creator and God outside the creation. He who blends with the higher Self becomes one with God the Creator and can understand the mysteries of creation. But he who separates even from the higher Self can go beyond time and blend with the God outside creation.

"This, I think, is what constitutes real success."

Notes & Bibliography

1. Frankl, V.E., The Doctor and the Soul (New York: Alfred A. Knopf, 1955).
2. In this book the word Man (with capital M) is used to designate the species *Homo sapiens*; man (lower case) is used for a male member of the species.
3. Wilson, C., *The Outsider* (Boston: Houghton Mifflin, 1956).
4. James, W., *The Varieties of Religious Experience* (London: Longman's, Green and Co. 1902).

5. Newman, J.H., *Apologia pro Vita Sua* (London: Longman's and Co. 1864).
6. Ouspensky, P.D., *A New Model of the Universe* (London: Kegan Paul, Trench, Trubner and Co., 1934).
7. Tillich, P., *The Courage to Be* p.147 (New Haven: Yale University Press 1952).
8. *Gurdjieff, Ouspensky and the System*. When I met Gurdjieff in New York City in 1948 he was already approaching the end of his life. He was living in a way which was obviously very unhealthy both for himself and for his "tail of donkey" (a phrase he used when referring to his followers). Members of the "tail" were crowded into the rather small room he used for his meetings in the Wellington Hotel. The air was thick with tobacco smoke and alcohol fumes. Readings either from *Beelzebub's Tales* or *Fragments* went on interminably. The food at supper was, for my poor stomach, indigestible. The endless toasts to the various categories of idiots drunk in Armagnac made my head swim. Worst of all was the atmosphere of concentrated guru worship that pervaded the assembly. As one cynical observer put it, "They seem to be having a competition to see who can kiss Gurdjieff's ass most obsequiously".

All this resulted in a negative reaction on my part. "If this is really the way to awakening I'd just as soon remain asleep."

Gurdjieff and Ouspensky both adopted unhealthy life styles. Both treated their physical bodies very badly. Both smoked which, in view of my personal loathing of the tobacco habit, seemed to me a serious defect. In spite of which I feel enormously indebted to them both. Had it not been for the support offered by the System at a certain critical moment in my life I would probably have "left the theater" in my early twenties. The System offered me a way out of the Abyss of Meaninglessness. It gave me a valid life aim without which life was worthless.

For many years I fed on the ideas of the System. Ideas carry enormous power and can entirely alter the shape of people's lives. Ideas can launch crusades, start wars, save people, destroy people, build civilizations or wreck them. Ideas form an important part of the Lattice of Karma of any man or woman who lives above the animal level.

So what about the System? Is it dead? And what about the bringer of the System, that "great enigma", *Mister* G. Gurdjieff? Was he an avatar, an incarnation of the highest aspect of the Mind Force? Was he a magician-hypnotist who used his powers for his own profit? Was he a behavioral psychologist who experimented with humans rather than rats? Was he just one more player of the "world's oldest con game", offering a new religion to true Believers in exchange for their worship and a considerable flow of cash?

Perhaps he was all these things — and more. One thing is certain. He possessed a certain something that set him apart from the ordinary run of human beings. In this age of the mass-man, when humans seem increasingly to resemble articulated dolls stamped out of sheets of plastic by computerized robots, he was unique. Looking at him as he sat there, his red fez on his bald head, playing weird melodies on his lap organ, the impression struck me that this was a king in exile who belonged to a different, more heroic age, a ruler of men forced to wear a humble disguise and to move unrecognized among the plastic dolls.

A king he undoubtedly was, nor could one have any doubts about his state of exile. Like his "Mr. Beelzebub" he was "far from the place of his arising". But was he, as his followers are fond of asserting, a great teacher? Perhaps he was for a few, a *very* few. Those few constituted a small group of men and women strong enough and self-reliant enough not to be completely dominated by the aura of power that surrounded Gurdjieff.

J.G. Bennett, in his book *Gurdjieff: A Very Great Enigma* (Coombe Springs Press, 1963) has given to this power the name *hvareno* , a word taken from old Zoroastrian teachings. It could be translated as "the royal touch" or "kingly power". Does possession of this power make a man or woman a great teacher? Not necessarily. In fact it may very well turn its possessor into a very bad teacher. These natural kings move among ordinary men and women as a wolf moves through a flock of sheep. It takes a very high level of self-control if that wolf is to resist the temptation to take a nip now and then out of the hides of the poor wooly fools with which he finds himself surrounded.

Now Gurdjieff is dead. Ouspensky is dead. Bennett is dead. One by one the members of the old circle have fallen by the way. What about "the System"? Is it also dead?

The answer I give to this question is yes. It is dead in the rigid forms which various commentators have given it. It is dead in the "Ouspenskian Version" (published as *In Search of the Miraculous*). It is dead in the "Oragean Version" (published privately by C. Daly King). It is dead in the "Bennett Version", formulated mainly in *Gurdjieff: Making a New World* (London: Turnstone Books, 1973).

But what about the "Gurdjieffian version" of the System? Is that also dead?

It is not, for the simple reason that Gurdjieff never published a System. He used instead the traditional Sufi method of transmitting ideas by the Teaching Story (see Idries Shah, *A Perfumed Scorpion*, London: The Octagon Press, 1978).

Both Gurdjieff's books, *Beelzebub's Tales to his Grandson* and *Meetings with Remarkable Men* (New York: E.P. Dutton and Co., 1969) are collections of Teaching Stories. By presenting the material in this way Gurdjieff avoided fossilizing the teachings in rigid forms like the dogmas of the church. A Teaching Story may have many interpretations and contain meanings at many different levels. To find the hidden meanings the student has to abandon his or her habitual patterns of thinking and learn to think in other categories.

This is illustrated by the famous Teaching Story called *The Elephant in the Dark*. Each of the sages who examined the elephant in the dark formed a different idea of what the beast was like. The one who grabbed its tail said it resembled a rope. The one who took hold of its leg thought it resembled a pillar and so on. So each sage published his own version of the elephant. There was the "tail version", the "leg version", the "trunk version". The real form of the elephant eluded them all because, to see the elephant as a whole, one had to turn on the light. This was exactly what the examining sages could not do (see *The Elephant in the Dark*, Leonard Lewin, editor, New York: E.P. Dutton and Co., 1976).

9. Ouspensky, P.D., *In Search of the Miraculous*, p. 85 (New York: Harcourt, Brace and Co., 1949).
10. For a discussion of the role of the Masters in Theosophy see Campbell, B.F., *Ancient Wisdom Revived* p. 53 (Berkeley, CA.: Univ. California Press, 1980).

11. "But *two hundred conscious people*, if they existed and if they found it necessary and legitimate, could change the whole of life on the earth." This from Gurdjieff (*In Search of the Miraculous* p. 310) Was he serious? Surely not. For further discussion of the role played by members of the inner circle see Bennett, J.G., *The Masters of Wisdom* (London: Turnstone Books, 1977) and Scott, E. *The People of the Secret* (London: The Octagon Press, 1983).

12. The gnostics and the scientists have different attitudes toward Nature. Scientists tend to think that they can compel Nature to reveal her secrets by brute force. This attitude is best exemplified by the gigantic atom smashers. At the cost of millions of dollars these vast machines are expected to reveal the *superforce* as it existed in the first instant of creation. To the gnostic this expenditure of energy and money seems hopelessly misplaced. Nature can never be forced to reveal her really important secrets, which don't relate to the superforce anyway. Goethe, who was a gnostic as well as a scientist, expressed this idea in *Faust*. Though Faust was a seeker of secrets he understood the limitations imposed on him by the force that had created him.

"Full of secrets in broad daylight, Nature won't let herself be robbed of her veils. That which she does not reveal to your soul you won't force out of her with screws and levers." (*Faust*, Part I, scene 1.)

13. Jung, C.G., *Memories, Dreams, Reflections* (New York: Random House, 1961) see also Hoeller, S.A., *The Gnostic Jung* (Wheaton, Ill. The Theosophical Publishing House, 1982).
14. For a full account of the ideas of the proto-gnostics see Jonas, H., *The Gnostic Religion* (Boston: Beacon Press, 1963).
15. Quoted in Jastrow, R., *God and the Astronomers* (New York: Warner Books, 1984), p. 135.
16. The last proto-gnostics in Europe were the Cathars. Over 200 of them were burnt as heretics in a single bonfire below the castle of Montsegur in France in 1244. That pretty well destroyed gnosticism in Europe until the neo-gnostics emerged after the French Revolution.
17. For *The Gospel of Truth* see Robinson, J.M., *The Nag Hammadi Library* (New York: Harper and Row, 1977).
18. *The Bhagavad Gita* chapter 9, verse 7 and 8. Nikhilananda translator, (New York: Ramakrishna-Vivekananda Center, 1944).
19. *ibid.*, chapter 3, verse 27.
20. *The Katha Upanishad* from *The Thirteen Principal Upanishads*, Hume, R.E., translator (London: Humphrey Milford, 1934) rearranged.
21. Quoted in Gore, R., "The Once and Future Universe", *National Geographic* vol. 163, #6, p. 704, 1983.
22. Genesis 1: 2,3.

23. For Ouspensky's comments on this saying see *In Search of the Miraculous*, p. 95.
24. Pais, A., *Subtle is the Lord* (New York: Oxford U.P., 1982).
25. Quoted in Davies, P., *Superforce* (New York: Simon and Schuster, 1984). Not all physicists agree that the universe is pointless. Thus Davies, in the above book, concludes: "The laws which enable the universe to come into being spontaneously seem themselves to be the product of exceedingly ingenious design. If physics is the product of design the universe must have a purpose, and the evidence of modern physics suggests strongly to me that the purpose includes us." (p. 243).
26. *Superforce*, p. 181.
27. For an overall picture of the modern theory of creation see Calder, N., *Timescale* (New York: The Viking Press, 1983).
28. Crick, F., *Life Itself* (New York: Simon and Schuster, 1981).
29. For the role played by morphogenetic fields in evolution see Sheldrake, R., *A New Science of Life* (Los Angeles: J.P. Tarcher, 1981). Sheldrake is willing to admit that, in the course of evolution, new morphic units, together with their morphogenetic fields, must have come into being. This might be ascribed to "the creative activity of an agency pervading and transcending nature; or to blind and purposeless chance." (p. 150). A cautious scientist, he sidesteps the problem. "...a choice

between these metaphysical possibilities could never be made on the basis of any empirically testable scientific hypothesis".

30. For a fuller explanation of the concept of holons see Koestler, *The Ghost in the Machine*, (New York: The Macmillan Co., 1967), p.341.

31. It is difficult to overestimate the spiritual harm that neo-Darwinism has inflicted. Arthur Koestler, in the above book, describes it as one of the "Four Pillars of Unwisdom" and that description is fully justified. Here we have a dogmatic assertion by scientists, who are in no position to prove the correctness of their theory, that every living structure, no matter how complex, resulted from purely random mutations sorted out by natural selection. This leads to the conclusion that the life process has no purpose, that the whole universe is mindless and operates as randomly as a roulette wheel. "If a group of monkeys danced on typewriters long enough they would, purely by chance, write all the books of the Bible." This is the sort of thing that passes for reasoning among the neo-Darwinians. They forget that the odds against such an event happening by chance are so enormous that, to produce it, those monkeys would have to dance for a time longer than the age of the universe. One might as well argue that, by throwing bricks around at random, one would sooner or later end up with a well constructed house. For a fuller discussion of this subject see Taylor, G.R., *The Great Evolution Mystery* (New York: Harper and Row, 1983).

32. Brand, S., *The Next Whole Earth Catalog* (San Francisco, CA.: Point, 1981).
33. Lovelock, J.E., *Gaia* (Oxford: Oxford U.P., 1979).
34. *Homo sapiens sapiens*. This double emphasis on the wisdom of our species must seem to some observers doubly unjustified. The second sapiens has been added by over zealous taxonomists to distinguish modern Man from his more massive relative, *Homo sapiens neanderthalensis* who appears to have become extinct.
35. Swift, J., *Gulliver's Travels*. It is odd to think that this savage satire was, in the days of my youth, considered a suitable book for children (maybe still is).
36. Gurdjieff, G., *All and Everything* (New York: Harcourt, Brace and Co., 1950).
37. Koestler, A., *op. cit.*
38. Hesse, H., *The Journey to the East* (New York: The Noonday Press, 1956).
39. Quoted in *Views from the Real World : Early Talks with Gurdjieff* (New York: E.P. Dutton and Co., 1973), p. 250.
40. For the allegory of the Deputy Steward see *In Search of the Miraculous*, p. 60. The function of the Observer has been described by Arthur J. Deikman in *The Observing Self* (Boston: Beacon Press, 1982).
41. de Ropp, R.S., *The Master Game* (New York: Delacorte Press, 1968).

42. *Chi* (which Gurdjieff calls *hanbledzoin*) has been called the life blood of the second body, the body *kesdjan*. This body, generated by conscious effort, envelops the first body as a field of force envelops a magnet.

The magician, the shaman, the sorcerer all develop this body but do not necessarily use it for beneficial purposes. It can be used destructively and often is.

Possession of a kesdjan body does not confer liberation on its possessor. Such a one will have climbed the Mountain of Power but still has to climb the Mountain of Liberation. It is easy to get stuck on the Mountain of Power.

A sorcerer is one who has developed this field of force but uses it for personal ends, to destroy enemies, attract women, get money. It is this misuse of the force that has given sorcery a bad name.

For this reason it is hard to understand why Carlos Castaneda describes his teacher, "Juan Matus", as a sorcerer. The old man Castaneda describes was not a sorcerer at all but a fairly skillful magician with a tendency to change into a college professor and to deliver lectures under such headings as "The Sorcerer's Explanation". This led Richard de Mille, in his brilliant analysis of the don Juan phenomenon, (*The Don Juan Papers*, Santa Barbara, CA.: Ross Erikson Publishers, 1980) to conclude that don Juan was a composite put together by his creator out of various bits and pieces. Don

Juan's teachings contained much that was of value but he was neither a sorcerer nor a Yaqui Indian. He existed only in the "separate reality" located in the mind of his creator in much the same way as Nietzsche's Zarathustra existed. Nietzsche, however, never managed to persuade the faculty of a major university to grant him a Ph.D. for his Zarathustra.

43. "Breathe consciously" (*hosh dar dam*) was the first of the eleven aphorisms of Khwaja Abd al Khaliq, adopted by the Naqshbandi dervishes as the basis of their practice. The aphorisms are given with comments by J.G. Bennett (*The Masters of Wisdom*, p.133). Breathing, Bennett declares, is the activity that nourishes the higher body, the vehicle called by Gurdjieff the *kesdjan* body. This nourishment is extracted only if the breath is taken attentively. Breath control formed the basis of the *zikr* of the Masters of Wisdom and they attributed their great longevity to this practice. Awareness of breathing was also used by the Christian Masters in the Syrian desert and is described in the *Philokalia*. (Kadloubovsky, E., and Palmer, G.E.H., translators. *Writings from the Philokalia on the Prayer of the Heart* London: Faber and Faber, 1951), p. 33.

44. Ram Dass (Richard Alpert), *Remember: Be Here Now* (San Cristobal, N.M.: Lama Foundation, 1971).

45. Viktor Frankl, originator of logotherapy, would probably include the will to meaning among

the higher wills. This is a difficult will to classify. One can make the world mean anything one wishes. The most fantastic myths have been and still are accepted by Believers because they give to the world a meaning that the Believer likes. For the gnostic the will to meaning is only valid if it is linked to the will to truth. Only then can it be trusted not to lead us into the realm of fantasy.

46. The allegory of the conveyance used by Gurdjieff is very old. Its significance was explained by Yama, King of the Dead, in the Katha Upanishad.

"Know then that the Higher Self rides in the chariot, the body is the chariot, the intellect is the charioteer and the mind the reins. The senses are the horses and the objects of the senses are the roads. He who has no understanding and whose mind is never firmly held his senses are unmanageable like the vicious horses of a charioteer. But he who has understanding and whose mind is always firmly held, his senses are under control like the good horses of a charioteer."

47. Sheldon, W.H., *The Varieties of Temperament* (New York: Harper Bros., 1942).

48. Kriegel, R. and M.H., *The C Zone* (New York: Doubleday and Co. 1984).

49. The relationship of the Higher Self to the ego was well expressed by Nietzsche's Zarathustra. "Behind your thoughts and feelings, my brother, there is a mighty Lord, an unknown

sage–it is called the Self: it dwells in your body, it is your body.

"Your Self laughs at your ego, and its proud prancings. 'What are these prancings and flights of thought to me?' it says to itself. 'A byway to my purpose. I am the leading string of the "I" and the prompter of its notions.'" *Thus Spake Zarathustra* (in *The Philosophy of Nietzsche*, The Modern Library, New York: Random House, no date, translator T. Common).

50. Gold, E.J., *Life in the Labyrinth* (Nevada City, CA.: Gateways/IDHHB Publishing, 1986).

51. A few words should be said on the subject of prognosis. This word is commonly used in connection with illness and refers to the process of estimating the course that a disease will take in the future. It was used long ago by "the Father of Medicine" as is shown by the following Hippocratic aphorism: *Declare the past, diagnose the present, prognose the future. As to disease, strive to do two things — to help, or at least do no harm.*

Prognosis may also be used by guides on the Way when they try to estimate the probability that a given seeker will make progress or become stuck in one of the many traps.

In this connection I have found useful a small group of poetic gems that I call "the gnostic limericks". The first two were devised, in whole or in part, by my one-time friend, Aldous Huxley. The third was transmitted to me by Alan Watts. (The original was in French). The authorship of the fourth is unknown to me.

I

The pious old man of Peoria,
Just to increase his sense of euphoria,
  Would don his tuxedo
  And murmur the credo
Along with the sanctus and gloria.

II

The muddled old man of Thermopolae
Could never do anything properly.
  He exhausted his days
  In a mystical maze
Acting sweetly serenely but sloppily.

III

A sprightly young cynic called Widgeon
Couldn't stomach the Christian religion.
  He asked, "How can God be
  This preposterous three,
A father, a son, and a pigeon?"

IV

An earnest young seeker called Sam
Said, "I think I've found out what I am.
  I'm a creature that moves
  In predestinate grooves.
I'm not even a bus. I'm a tram."

The prognoses are clear. The pious old man
of Peoria will assuredly become stuck in the
quagmire of ritual. He will indulge in dressing
up and murmuring magical formulae. There

are millions of such "pious old men". They swarm in all the organized religions, including Buddhism which, in view of the Buddha's disapproval of rituals, is rather surprising. The muddled old man of Thermopolae will also surely lose his way. He is not only hopelessly unpractical but also has a taste for what Gurdjieff called "cream from the navel of the estimable Scheherazade". In other words he will swallow any old tale. His credulity and suggestibility will infallibly lead him astray. He will wander around in a mystical maze, drifting from guru to guru, never really getting anywhere. In him the fantasy Work will infallibly take the place of the real Work.

The prognosis is somewhat better for the sprightly young cynic called Widgeon. He has used his intelligence to dismiss one of the myths that were tacked on to the original teachings of Jesus by the Fathers of the Church. These include not only the myth of "the preposterous three", but also the myth of the Immaculate Conception (which would have left Jesus with only 23 chromosomes instead of the 44 plus X and Y needed for the making of a complete human male) and the myth of the physical resurrection and ascent into heaven which violates the laws of both biology and physics. It is strange to think that millions of otherwise intelligent people still take these myths seriously.

The prognosis for Widgeon is nonetheless guarded. His cynicism will probably cause him to dismiss not only the absurd myths that have been added to the teachings of Jesus but also the teachings themselves. So Widgeon's cynicism may prove to be an obstacle in his way.

The prognosis is better for the earnest young seeker called Sam. Sam has confronted a great truth. He knows he is programmed. He has come face to face with the fact of his own mechanicalness. This may not seem like much of an accomplishment but it is a beginning. Only he who has confronted the fact of his mechanicalness can hope to find his way to real inner freedom.

52. For a literary example of the unlawful use of violent methods see Fowles, J., *The Magus* (New York: Dell Publishing Co., 1969). This curious fantasy portrays a "Magus", Maurice Conchis, who bases his teaching method on the "theater of life", in which the notions of proscenium, stage, auditorium, audience, actors are all discarded. All the members of his group are actors, improvising the drama as they go along. This method of teaching is quite lawful though very difficult.

Conchis's enterprise took a turn onto the left hand path when the subject of his experiment, Nicholas Urfe, was kidnapped and forced, very much against his will, to go through a trial that publicly exposed his fundamental weaknesses.

This is certainly one way of forcing a person to confront his or her buffers, but it is a very dangerous method. In this case it was doubly unlawful because Nicholas Urfe had not agreed to take part in the experiment.

So, although Maurice Conchis is portrayed as a Master with quite unusual powers, it is hard for a discriminating reader to decide just what he is trying to do. He was apparently one very mixed up Magus who broke all the rules of the game, endangered the sanity and even the life of the subjects of his experiments and in general seemed not to know his left hand from his right.

53. Idries Shah, *Caravan of Dreams* (London: Octagon Press, 1968), p. 202.
54. For a fuller account of the function of buffers see *In Search of the Miraculous* , p. 154.
55. Idries Shah, *op. cit.* , p. 200.
56. Genesis 6: 19-22.
57. Khayyam, Omar, *Rubaiyat* , quatrains 73 and 74, Edward Fitzgerald's translation.

Index

Dear Reader of Self-Completion:

If you are one of those intrepid voyagers who has not only purchased Mr. de Ropp's book (or acquired it in some other way, upon which we will not speculate here), but also read his ideas with full attention, you may be interested in further explorations along this line.

For referral to other books and study materials directed towards the Work, as opposed to the fantasy work, you may contact Gateways at the address and phone below with no obligation to purchase.

Ask for a free catalog of books currently available to the trade and, should you wish to voyage further, a listing of private publications.

Gateways Books and Tapes
PO Box 370
Nevada City, CA 95959
(916) 477-1116